MW00788660

THE
GALVESTON
BUCCANEERS

THE GALVESTON BUCCANEERS

SHEARN MOODY AND THE 1934 TEXAS LEAGUE CHAMPIONSHIP

KRIS RUTHERFORD

Foreword by E. Douglas McLeod

THE
History
PRESS

Published by The History Press
Charleston, SC 29403
www.historypress.net

Copyright © 2015 by Kris Rutherford
All rights reserved

Front cover, bottom: Moody Stadium. *Courtesy of E. Douglas McLeod/Moody Archive.*
Back cover: Images of Buck Fausett courtesy of Robert J. Fausett.

Opposite: Courtesy of Karen Rutherford.

First published 2015

ISBN 9781540212801

Library of Congress Control Number: 2015942732

Notice: The information in this book is true and complete to the best of our knowledge. It is offered without guarantee on the part of the author or The History Press. The author and The History Press disclaim all liability in connection with the use of this book.

All rights reserved. No part of this book may be reproduced or transmitted in any form whatsoever without prior written permission from the publisher except in the case of brief quotations embodied in critical articles and reviews.

In memory of Stan Elbert,
a Knothole Gang original (1920–2015)

CONTENTS

FOREWORD

Countless sagas have been written about the city of Galveston, located in the Gulf of Mexico and connected to the rest of Texas by a forever bridge and a state-run ferry service. Readers are fascinated by colorful tales of the thirty-two-mile-long, two-mile-wide barrier island an hour's drive from Houston whose state has sworn allegiance to six flags under Spain, France, Mexico, the Texas Republic, the Confederate States of America and the United States. Rugged "Born on the Island" Galvestonians (BOIs) would have visitors believe there should have been a seventh flag, that of the Independent Principality or Empire of Galveston. After all, there truly were BOIs who at one time in the island's past had never ventured across the causeway bridge to the mainland of Texas. Galveston was the whole world to them, and they had no interest in horizons beyond.

Who would not be enthralled with the island's history over the past five hundred years? Here were shipwrecked Spanish explorers; fierce, cannibalistic Karankawa Indians; Texas Revolutionary armies; Civil War battles; spectacular financial empires built and lost; great fires and hurricanes; yellow fever epidemics; immigration stations prior to Ellis Island; expansive port and maritime industries; King Cotton and Queen Sugar; and organized vice—of immense interest to most, the bootlegging and gambling era of Galveston and more. But wait! This is a baseball book about Shearn Moody and his Buccaneers, is it not? It is, yes, but author Kris Rutherford has captured a story about baseball in a very unique city, in a very unique era and about some very unique people therein. Baseball fans and history buffs alike will love this book. Old-timers on this island who remember the Buccaneers and the 1930s will especially adore it.

The Enigmatic Moody Family

I was born in Galveston in 1941, five years after Shearn Moody died. When very young, my four siblings and I knew the very private Moodys, but not very well. My great-grandfather Alexander (Alec) Douglas Milroy, whose home still stands at 701 Broadway, was a cotton man and banked with W.L. (Will) Moody Jr., and Will talked Alec into buying some ANICO stock in the early 1900s—a smart move, I must say, for later generations of McLeods. When I was ten years old, my ever-gracious mother introduced me to Mr. Moody, then eighty-five years old, at the Galvez Club. Whenever he saw my mother, he always teased her about how frugal my Scottish great-grandfather Alec was and how hard it was to talk him into buying that ANICO stock. I also knew Robert L. Moody and Shearn Moody Jr. by sight, six and eight years older than I was, respectively; however, they were sent off to military school as little boys, so we saw them just occasionally during the holidays.

Treasure Island

Galveston was a wondrous and mysterious place for kids to grow up in the 1940s and 1950s. World War II German prisoners were quartered at Fort Crockett, two blocks from our home, and the older kids convinced the little ones that the mean Nazis were coming to get us. For the children of Denver Court, it was a time of beachcombing, fishing at Lake Como, playing in the summer barefoot in little more than our underwear, sandlot baseball and football, watching the old Gulf Coast League White Caps hit a few homers on balmy nights, savoring the best and freshest seafood in the nation and getting in trouble with an array of BB guns, illegal big firecrackers and—in our teenage years—hot rods and motor bikes.

To the Rescue of Our Island's Youth

King Cotton provided summer employment for boys willing to work. At that time, the Port of Galveston was a giant exporter of cotton, which generated many jobs for men and women, as well as industrious students on vacation. In high school, my brother worked summers at the Moody Cotton Compress, and I worked for four summers at the H. Kempner Cotton Company at Thirty-eighth and Wharf. Hard labor is good for a growing boy, but while in college, I "wised up" and had the good fortune of spending my summers as a lifeguard at one of the premier Moody hotels (where I became acquainted firsthand with the Moody boys, then aspiring young businessmen). I often took direct supervision from Robert Moody, who throughout his long and successful career was a no-nonsense, hands-on entrepreneur. Fifty plus years later, I am still with those good folks and have therefore learned from the family and from longtime associates facts versus fiction about the Moodys of Galveston.

The Billionaire Moodys

Members of the Moody family were generally publicity shy, and thus books critical of them often did not contain "their side of the story." In other words, they likely were never interviewed. In *The Galveston Buccaneers*, Kris Rutherford was determined to write only factual information, and where critics differed, he aired all viewpoints in an interesting way for his readers. In conclusion, and notwithstanding the immense knowledge I previously had accumulated about the Moodys of Galveston, I so enjoyed learning much more about Shearn Moody from Mr. Rutherford's book. The BOIs will likely agree that he captured Shearn's persona perfectly.

E. Douglas McLeod, JD, LLM
Attorney and Counselor at Law

PREFACE

This project began as an effort to chronicle the magical summer of 1934, when Galveston's most successful Texas League baseball team claimed its first statewide championship since 1899. Yet along the way, I made contact with some remarkable people who offered information and research leads enabling me to discover a tremendous amount of information that never made its way into the newspapers. After many telephone conversations, face-to-face meetings and e-mails, it became apparent the story of the 1934 Galveston Buccaneers didn't begin during spring training, and it didn't end in September. The people I had the fortune of meeting during this effort helped craft a story beginning over a century earlier than planned. Likewise, many facts learned along the way allowed me to discover interesting comparisons between the lives of two men who came from seemingly different worlds but were destined to help bring the long-awaited championship to Galveston.

I wish to thank many people for their participation and assistance during the eighteen months of research culminating in this book. Doug McLeod, a former Texas state representative and longtime Moody family associate, offered undocumented information about the Moodys of the early twentieth century and arranged access to volumes of family photographs that helped bring the complete story into focus. I also want to express my gratitude to Bobby Moody Jr., whose interest in this project about the grandfather he never knew provided the fuel to transform this baseball story into one encompassing far more than merely a sport.

PREFACE

I also had the pleasure of conversing with several children and grandchildren of former players over the last year, most notably Robert Fausett, grandson of former Buccaneer Buck Fausett. Robert graciously offered a tremendous amount of information about his grandfather's life, as well as access to family scrapbooks containing invaluable photographs and news clippings of his baseball career. Likewise, Dianne Bell Sides and Mary Bell Mowlam offered insight into and photographs of their father, Buccaneer star outfielder Beau Bell. Also, Mary Van Fleet Williams, daughter of former *Galveston Daily News* sports editor Bill Van Fleet, shared what she knew of her father's days covering the Buccaneers. Finally, Stan Elbert, an original member of the Buccaneers fan club as an eleven-year-old, shared his memories of the team and attending games at Moody Stadium.

As always, when researching any aspect of Texas League history, Scott Hanzelka and league president Tom Kayser provided leads to a wealth of information, as well as photographs from the Texas League archives. Furthermore, the Rosenberg Library in Galveston, in particular Travis Bible, assisted in obtaining important information buried in the archives of the Center for Galveston and Texas History.

Finally, I wish to thank my wife, traveling companion and photographer, Karen Rutherford, for putting up with me throughout this effort, as well as my son Kolton, who assisted with Internet research and took notes during many days on the road through East Texas. Without their patience, as well as that of my other children, Kristianna and Klayton, this project would have never transformed from what initially may have been an extended article into a book-length work.

INTRODUCTION

Galveston, Texas, September 25, 1934

They began arriving early on Tuesday morning. A handful of people gathered even before Roy Koehler called the front desk of the Buccaneer, the grandest of Galveston's hotels, from San Antonio's MoPac Railroad Depot. An eleven-story structure completed in 1929, the Buccaneer had become the pride of the Galveston-based National Hotel Company. With deluxe suites, parlors, elevators, game rooms and an indoor putting green, the hotel had been the brainchild of Shearn Moody, the dashingly handsome heir apparent to the Moody family fortune and its business interests in Galveston and nationwide. In the mid-1920s, before Galveston became a national tourist attraction, the thirty-year-old businessman predicted tourism's importance to the city's future and convinced his father, W.L. Moody Jr., to invest in the burgeoning industry.

Upon opening, the Buccaneer became the premier site for upscale lodging, conventions and other events in Galveston, providing accommodations for famous entertainers, including Guy Lombardo, Benny Goodman and the Glenn Miller Band. Rather than entertain at the hotel, though, celebrities normally appeared at Sam Maceo's Balinese Ballroom or Hollywood Club along Seawall Boulevard. Maceo built his clubs into Galveston's most popular attractions, each a hub for vice crimes, including gambling, prostitution and alcohol in the Prohibition era. Though the Moodys and Maceos didn't associate publicly, both profited from the other's business. Sam Maceo's clientele stayed in the Moody hotels, and hotel conventioneers engaged in Galveston's nightlife after hours. Local law enforcement did little to interfere with Maceo's business; after all, he helped bring prosperity to the island during the early years of the Great Depression and employed over 10 percent of Galveston's population. With Prohibition ending in late 1933, the product around which Maceo had built his business became legal. Still, gambling remained taboo, and the Maceo casinos provided entertainment for visitors and islanders alike. On this morning, only the high-stakes gamblers counted cash. Just a few hours earlier, Galveston achieved a goal the entire city had been waiting for since 1899.

By 9:00 a.m., the Buccaneer lobby had reached full capacity, the crowd overflowing onto Seawall Boulevard. Shouts and cheers, along with the woodwinds, brass and percussion of the local Shrine Band and Boys Booster Band, drowned the persistent roar of the Gulf of Mexico's pounding surf just a few yards to the east. The crowd soon topped three thousand people, with men, women and children anxiously awaiting the hometown heroes' arrival.

Schoolboys either skipping or dismissed from classes grew impatient as the wait dragged on, particularly members of the Knothole gang. Stan Elbert, among the first to join the club in 1931, strolled through the crowd awaiting a celebration four years in the making. As 9:40 a.m. approached, people jammed Seawall Boulevard in hopes of catching a glimpse of Galveston's newest celebrities: the Galveston Buccaneers, 1934 Texas League Baseball champions.

Arriving at Union Station on the eastern end of Strand Avenue, the Buccaneers hurriedly disembarked the passenger train and made their way through a crowd two blocks long and ten people deep. Eventually, they piled into automobiles waiting to shuttle them to the celebration on Seawall Boulevard. Many remained soaked with whatever beverage the team had celebrated with on the train ride; even the well-dressed secretary, Sam Jack Evans, was no exception. Buccaneer vice-president Roy Koehler emerged from the train wearing what remained of his derby hat, a formerly handsome piece of headwear that had not survived the celebration intact.

As the parade traveled along Galveston's streets, Buck Fausett, Beau Bell, Wally Moses, Charlie English and the previous evening's pitching hero, Harry Gumbert, anxiously awaited a welcome home party. Many Buccaneer players had been strangers when new manager Billy Webb assembled training camp in March, but in the six months since, they had gelled as a team and defeated the San Antonio Missions, the same team they had lost to a year earlier, for the championship. Southern Association champion New Orleans Pelicans remained to be played in the Dixie Series. But on this morning, the Buccaneers prepared to celebrate with the fans who had supported them all season despite the sportswriters, gamblers and baseball experts' persistent predictions that Galveston was incapable of bringing home the Texas League Championship.

When the parade arrived at the Buccaneer, admirers mobbed the players. While Texas League All-Star third-baseman Buck Fausett greeted his wife and infant son, others signed autographs and enjoyed congratulatory pats on the back. Manager Billy Webb and team owner Shearn Moody appeared on the grand staircase of the hotel lobby, this day doubling as a podium.

With the crowd still buzzing, Moody read a telegram received from Texas League president J. Alvin Gardner: "Congratulations on your first pennant. Now for the championship of Dixie for you and the fine fans of Galveston!"

Then, from L.C. McEvoy, president of the St. Louis Browns: "Sincerest congratulations to you and manager Billy Webb and all players. Your club's aggressive uphill battle during the latter part of the season stamps them real champions and worthy participants in the Dixie Series, from which we confidently expect them to bring victory to the Texas League."

A roar rose in the lobby as fans offered their well wishes. Indeed, the morning's celebration would be short-lived, with the opening pitch of the Dixie Series less than thirty-six hours away. Billy Webb thanked all of Galveston for its support through the long season and received deafening applause when he predicted that the Buccaneers would make short work of the Pelicans.

After Moody and Webb stepped away from the microphone, the crowd slowly dispersed, many making their way to Moody Stadium in hopes of purchasing Dixie Series tickets. Others remained behind to enjoy the moment. Not only had the Buccaneers brought the city its first statewide baseball championship in thirty-five years, but the win also created a sense of achievement not arising from the ashes of economic downturn, disease, mass destruction and death that had defined Galveston since the first Europeans set foot on the island four centuries earlier. The older residents—the really old-timers born on the island and living through its best and worst days—felt a sense of satisfaction sweep over Galveston, a feeling many thought would never return after the glorious days of the late nineteenth century and their sudden, deadly end in the late summer of 1900.

1
LAYING THE CORNERSTONE

At the dawn of the twentieth century, few would believe Galveston, Texas, and Grant County, Arkansas, had anything in common. The Gulf of Mexico surrounded Galveston Island, the commercial center of Texas, and Strand Avenue, hailed by many as the "Wall Street of the Southwest." Galveston bustled with activity, much of it on wharves where workers offloaded ships holding products bound for inland Texas. While the ships may have come to Galveston for any number of products, most came with orders to return with one commodity: cotton.

Cotton had long been the key to economic survival in the southern United States, and since the Civil War, Galveston's development allowed Texas cotton growers to capitalize on the industry. The only Class One port on the Gulf Coast, Galveston rivaled New Orleans in terms of shipping, a city dominating southern commerce during the first six decades of the nineteenth century. But when Texas achieved independence from Mexico in 1836, settlers flooded the state, and Galveston took center stage. Texas cotton production grew exponentially in the mid-1800s, as cotton traders and cattle barons fought for supremacy in the state's burgeoning economy. Enormous cattle drives through central Texas to markets in Kansas and Chicago took a backseat to the annual cotton harvest as small family farms and plantation-like operations sent their crops overland to Galveston, just two miles off the Texas mainland. As shipments arrived, dozens of traders lined the wharves, shouting bids for a precious worldwide commodity.

As Galveston grew into the third-busiest port in the world, four hundred miles northeast, many in Arkansas' Grant County lived in poverty. On the edge of the state's West Gulf Coastal Plain region, landlocked Grant County lay just west of Arkansas' most fertile region, the Mississippi River Delta. About thirty miles south of Little Rock, the county had a plentiful supply of a slow-growing timber, but more than a few farmers cleared forty-acre plots to grab a share of "King Cotton," the only cash crop grown. In Galveston, workers used modern industrial equipment to press cotton into bales and load them onto ships. In Grant County, on the other hand, most people survived with an axe, a team of mules and a single-furrow plow. Galveston gained fame as a city of firsts in Texas, setting the bar with urban improvements, including electricity, telephones and mail delivery. Grant County and its seven thousand residents, on the other hand, seemed shut off from conveniences emerging across the nation.

No one could have predicted that Galveston and Grant County were on a collision course—one that would destroy a grand city and send an impoverished region into even deeper despair. Ironically, the destructive forces also set the stage for what many considered Galveston's greatest day since 1899, when two men from different worlds helped a thirty-five-year-old Galveston dream come true.

Some Texas League historians mark the origin of the 1934 Texas League champions as January 1931, when Shearn Moody purchased the Waco Cubs and relocated the team to Galveston. For others, the Buccaneers didn't become a force until 1933, when Moody hired novice manager Billy Webb to replace Del Pratt after two unsuccessful seasons. Still others consider the key to the 1934 season as coming a decade earlier, when future Buccaneer stars like Buck Fausett, Beau Bell and Charlie English honed their skills on crude inner-city sandlot diamonds, university campuses and rural pastures. In reality, though, destiny laid the cornerstone of Galveston's 1934 success over a century earlier—in Essex County, Virginia.

William Lewis Moody was born on May 19, 1828, the second of five sons of Jameson and Mary Lankford Moody and grandson to Virginia landowner Lewis Moody and Revolutionary War veteran William Lankford. With Virginia home to some of the young nation's most respected universities, Moody learned to value education as a child, eventually enrolling in the

University of Virginia Law School in 1847. He could have established a law practice in his home state, but Moody understood the law of supply and demand as well any subject covered on the bar exam. Mid-nineteenth-century Virginia teemed with lawyers, so upon graduating in 1851, William sought a less competitive location. Texas, admitted to the Union only six years earlier, seemed primed for a population explosion.

William Moody traveled overland and on steamboat routes, arriving in Galveston, Texas, in the fall of 1851. His sights set on the small city of Dallas, Moody traveled northward on horseback through Houston, essentially paralleling today's Interstate 45. But some eighty miles south of Dallas, his horse pulled up lame and died near the small settlement of Fairfield in Freestone County. Virtually penniless, rather than continuing to Dallas by foot, William befriended a local merchant who financed his law practice in return for reading and writing lessons. Later, the merchant boasted that he was the only illiterate owner of a law practice in Texas.

Moody didn't find life as an attorney in Fairfield lucrative. He realized his financier's mercantile business offered chances for far greater wealth in a much shorter time. Moody soon opened a similar business of his own, experiencing enough success to send for his brothers George and David to join him in Texas. Together, the three established W.L. Moody and Brothers Company. The company met moderate success, but the threat of Civil War soon placed its future in peril.

Moody recognized the cotton industry's importance to Texas's future and his business. Likewise, he realized the industry couldn't thrive without slavery. When Freestone County voted 585–3 in favor of secession, Moody joined the Rebel cause, helping to organize the Texas Seventh Cavalry, Company G. He and his unit soon left Texas to join the fight east of the Mississippi River.

Moody's first stint as a soldier didn't last long. Months after reaching Tennessee, Union forces captured him at the Battle of Fort Donelson but soon released him in a prisoner exchange. Moody returned to Texas, but as an early indication that a Moody man was at his finest under pressure, he returned to battle in early 1863, defending Vicksburg, a city considered key to controlling the Mississippi River. Cited for bravery at the nearby Battle of Raymond, Moody suffered a serious injury during Vicksburg's ultimate fall into Union hands. Again, he returned to Texas, this time taking command of the Austin garrison for the remainder of the war.

After Robert E. Lee's surrender, W.L. Moody returned to Freestone County but soon decided Fairfield lacked the growth potential that W.L.

Colonel William Lewis Moody Sr. *Courtesy of E. Douglas McLeod/ Moody Archives.*

Moody and Brothers Company needed to thrive. When his brother David returned to Virginia, William moved the business to Galveston, the same port city where he had arrived in Texas fifteen years earlier. The reunited country, forthcoming Reconstruction period and Galveston's rapidly growing port seemed a prime market for Moody's ambitions. He sold his small but stately Fairfield home to his father-in-law for $2,800 and moved his wife and newborn son, William Lewis Jr., to the Texas coast. Here, he would make his mark on the economic history of Texas and the United States.

When the Moodys arrived in Galveston in 1866, William found the city's war recovery effort well underway. Galveston's growing cotton trade attracted buyers from across Texas and the Southeast to bid on raw materials that

The W.L. Moody Company's faded name can still be seen on the side of the Moody Building on the Strand in Galveston. *Karen Rutherford.*

farmers sent to the island for ginning, compressing and shipping. New steam-powered compresses soon allowed local workers to process 250 bales of cotton a day. The resourceful Moody joined in establishing Galveston as the country's leading cotton exporter, accepting growers' harvests on consignment and selling them to textile representatives lining Galveston's wharves.

As a cotton factor, Moody developed a keen understanding of commodity futures. By 1871, he had paid for cotton before the planting season, holding liens on growers' property as collateral. As competition grew and some cotton merchants employed questionable tactics to gain an upper hand, Moody helped organize the Galveston Cotton Exchange to govern member practices. Following a year of lucrative success, he established a New York office for his business.

While W.L. Moody recognized the importance of slavery to Texas's cotton industry, the postwar Moody sought to partially offset its loss by improving shipping routes from inland Texas to Galveston's compresses. Houston officials discouraged rail development to Galveston in an effort to protect their own interests, but by the early 1870s, Moody was leading the city in attracting the Gulf, Colorado and Santa Fe Railroad. The direct link to landlocked cotton markets gave Galveston a great advantage over Houston, whose leaders seemed intent on monopolizing the cotton industry. By 1887, railroad workers had completed a route connecting Galveston to North Texas and Kansas City, completely bypassing Houston in swinging southwest of the city. The project featured a two-mile bridge, the longest of its kind in the world, linking Galveston to the mainland.

While transportation to Texas's interior held one key to Galveston's prosperity, Moody knew if large ships could not access the island's port, railroad development would never pay dividends. Captains of large ships found entry to Galveston Bay treacherous, its shallow waters and oyster beds a threat to rip the hull of any vessel drawing more than a few feet of water. Moody took a lead role in the harbor improvement effort, serving on the Deep Water Commission and testifying before Congress for federal assistance. After nearly a decade, Congress appropriated funding, and within a short time, Galveston became the most active cotton port in the United States. W.L. Moody led the fight for Galveston, and his success made him a very wealthy man. But one member of the Moody family felt the patriarch was a bit shortsighted in his concentration on the cotton industry.

As William Lewis Moody Jr., or Will, grew into a young man, he developed aspirations far beyond trading cotton, prodding his father to diversify company interests. Will's foresight laid the groundwork for what would become a family financial empire that remains synonymous with Galveston 180 years after his father's birth.

2
EARLY GAINS AND GROWING PAINS

The Moody family and baseball arrived in Galveston simultaneously. Abner Doubleday, a Union officer stationed in Galveston after the war, reportedly laid out a baseball diamond in a prairie near the future site of the Ursuline Convent. Though Doubleday may not have actually invented baseball, if legend is accurate, he did introduce the game to Galveston. A year later, San Jacinto Battlefield, where Sam Houston's ragtag militia had defeated Santa Anna's Mexican army three decades earlier, hosted the first recorded baseball game in Texas history.

On a spring afternoon in 1867, some Galveston residents participated in a clash between the Stonewalls and Robert E. Lees on the battleground a few miles inland from Galveston Bay. The Stonewalls ran over the Lees like Sam Houston's militia battered Santa Anna's troops. At game's end, the Lees suffered a humiliating 35–2 defeat, a score making any call for a rematch ring hollow. Despite the lopsided affair, baseball had officially arrived in Texas. For the next twenty years, the game remained an amateur affair until a group of team owners organized the Texas League of Professional Baseball Clubs.

Galvestonians take pride in being known as the "City of Firsts" in Texas. Considering Galveston served as the commercial center of the state until the twentieth century, it naturally rested on the cutting edge of social and industrial development. From post offices to newspapers, streetlights to telephones, private schools to orphanages and Catholic hospitals to Jewish congregations—all found their Texas beginnings in Galveston. The improvements seemed novel at first, but their impact soon moved to the mainland, and all of Texas followed Galveston's lead.

Galveston firsts included far more than infrastructure. Officials of the rapidly growing city surrounded with water recognized the need for recreational activities for those on the island. Traditional mid-nineteenth-century leisure pursuits such as gambling, saloons and brothels soon shared the island with parks, green space and a slowly emerging economic benefit: tourism.

While a number of factors kept Galveston from competing with Houston in terms of industrial development, the island offered something Houston could not: beaches. By the late 1800s, tourists were trickling to Galveston's shoreline, the streetcar system offering service from Strand Avenue to the beaches eighteen hours a day. Swimming became so popular that city officials enacted ordinances prohibiting nude bathing except during late-night hours. Bathhouses and hotels attracted visitors, along with circus acts, hot-air balloons, bicycling and sailing. Interest in spectator sports grew as well, particularly wrestling, cockfighting, tennis and horse racing. Although Texas banned boxing in 1891, Galveston allowed exhibitions, and local resident Jack Johnson trained there on his way to becoming the first African American world heavyweight champion. Sports became ingrained in island culture and, in the words of historian David McComb, offered the island "a bit of character."

Galveston's most popular spectator sport arrived in 1888 when the city fielded a baseball team in the inaugural Texas League. Though early attempts to establish a statewide professional baseball league proved difficult, the Galveston Sand Crabs became a fixture on the circuit. Gaining immediate popularity among residents, the Sand Crabs took four of nine Texas League championships between 1888 and 1899. The city's beachfront ballpark drew a steady group of spectators seeking an alternative to the beach, and the descriptions of Galveston that opposing players took home further increased the island's reputation as a "playground."

Galveston's earliest Texas League teams saw success in the standings, yet an asterisk always seemed attached. After the Sand Crabs finished in third place in 1888, William Works led the team for the next two seasons, taking consecutive league batting titles. Galveston won its first Texas League championship in 1890, in a season lasting only six weeks. The truncated schedule so disillusioned team owners that the league didn't reorganize for 1891.

A year later, the Texas League returned, led by baseball mogul John McCloskey, whose confidence in the state's potential to support professional baseball led to his unofficial title: "Father of the Texas League." Houston so dominated the schedule that the second-place Sand Crabs posted a losing record, finishing nineteen and a half games behind the champion Mud Cats. The lopsided pennant race devastated team owners financially, and the following financiers lacked interest in launching another campaign. By 1895, however, with its eyes set on quality ballplayers and an improved product, the Texas League had reformed with a full slate of eight teams.

Galveston fans experienced some of Texas's best professional baseball in the late 1890s, the Sand Crabs winning 141 games over the following two seasons. George Bristow carried the Sand Crabs in 1895, pitching the team to thirty of its seventy-two wins. William Works returned with his strong bat, but the quality of baseball had improved, and his .344 batting average placed him a full one hundred points behind the league's leading hitter. Without Works and Bristow on the 1896 roster, the Sand Crabs fielded a balanced lineup and rose in the standings, finishing twelve games behind the pesky Mud Cats.

In 1897, the San Antonio Bronchos ran away with the season's first half, but just as the Sand Crabs caught fire, San Antonio folded. William Nance finished as one of six Sand Crabs with batting over .300, carrying Galveston to a 31-13 record over the final eight weeks. Thanks to San Antonio's mid-season demise, Galveston took its second Texas League championship. The Sand Crabs returned a strong lineup in 1898 and claimed another pennant, though the Spanish-American War ended the season after only a month.

Dallas, along with the four South Texas cities of Galveston, Houston, San Antonio and Austin, made plans to relaunch the Texas League in 1899. Unable to interest other northern cities, Dallas dropped its bid, leaving the league with only four southern-based teams. Galveston dominated the first two months of competition. In an effort to reignite fan interest in the other three cities, owners voted to split the season into halves, the first- and second-half winners to meet for the championship. When Galveston charged out of the gate and took a commanding second-half lead, Austin folded. With only three active teams, the league collapsed a few days later, and Galveston was again declared champion.

THE GALVESTON BUCCANEERS

While Galveston closed out the nineteenth century on top in Texas professional baseball circles, the Texas League failed to reorganize in 1900 and 1901. Upon its 1902 return, owners confined the league to six North Texas cities and kept the same slate of cities the following year. South Texas set out on its own. Galveston constructed a new ball field, Auditorium Stadium, in an open space at Avenue Q and Twenty-seventh Street for the South Texas League's inaugural season.

Austin had always been fast to join and fast to abandon the Texas League, so South Texas's new circuit organized as a compact group of four teams: Galveston, Houston and Beaumont packaged closely on the coast, with San Antonio the most distant. The South Texas League one-upped its northern counterparts in achieving Class C professional status based on the populations of the four cities involved. With Dallas and Fort Worth the only sizeable North Texas cities, the northern circuit received only a Class D designation.

Players in both North and South Texas recognized the quality difference between the two leagues. South Texas teams offered more money, and as the season moved on, some of North Texas's best players abandoned their teams for higher salaries. South Texas also offered stronger competition, with the San Antonio Mustangs winning the pennant, just two and a half games ahead of Galveston. In 1904, the Sand Crabs took the league title after first-half winner Houston collapsed when ballpark issues sent the team on the road for its entire second-half schedule. Galveston, again taking advantage of another team's misfortune, posted a 40-13 record over the same period. The 1904 championship represented the city's fifth in twelve seasons of professional baseball. Owners rewarded the ball club and its faithful fans with Sportsman's Park, at Avenue Q and Forty-first Street. The Sand Crabs played there until 1911, when another stadium took its place on the east end of Tremont near the beach. Despite improved facilities, team owners couldn't build a winning ball club.

After two more unsuccessful seasons, in 1907 the northern and southern circuits merged, once again fielding a statewide league. For the next twenty seasons, Galveston played miserably, posting just four winning seasons and finishing in the upper half of the standings only twice. Its best chance at a pennant came in 1915. In the thick of the second-half chase, on August 15, the renamed Galveston Pirates found their ballpark and season destroyed when a hurricane struck the Galveston area. The 1916 team played respectably, but the Pirates ceased operations early the next year, their last-place ranking and World War I keeping fans away from Pirate Field. The following year, Galveston, like most cities in the country, didn't field a team, although the Texas League managed to remain active.

Galveston rejoined the Texas League in 1919, but owners signed few quality players. In 1920, the Pirates lost one hundred games, posting a winning percentage of just .329 and trailing champion Fort Worth by nearly fifty-nine and a half games. Little changed over the next four years, even after Hotel Galvez owner Phil Sanders sold the franchise to local clothing merchant Nelson Leopold. Hoping to bring back the glory years of the 1890s, Leopold revived the "Sand Crabs" moniker, but a name change did little to improve the team's fortunes. Between 1921 and 1924, Galveston finished at least twenty-six games out of first place each season. Even another new ballpark, Gulfview Park at the 2800 block of Avenue R½, couldn't stop the bleeding on the scoreboard, as the Sand Crabs won just sixty games in 1923.

Prior to the 1924 season, the *Galveston Daily News* (*GDN*) solicited fan suggestions to improve the Sand Crabs. Investing more money in players, increasing reserved seating, reorienting the ballpark based on sun angles and improving streetcar service to the stadium led the responses. Leopold took many suggestions to heart and invested in his ballpark. He increased playing field dimensions; provided a separate entrance for kids, who made up a rather rambunctious "Knothole Gang"; and increased security to separate box seat spectators from those who paid general admission. In what Leopold considered a service to African American fans, he relocated their segregated seating area so they could avoid walking past white spectators, believing the experience humiliated African American fans and kept them away from the ballpark. Not only did he believe further segregation benefited the minority population, but he also tossed a bone to those able to pay by constructing box seats in their area. He also lowered ticket prices to $1.10 a game for the best seats in the house and offered a season ticket package for $50.00. However the 1924 club performed on the field, Leopold planned to cash in at the ticket gate.

As the season approached, all of Galveston looked forward to a squad that *GDN* sportswriters labeled the best in years. With over 5,300 paid admissions, Leopold's club finished third in the league in opening day attendance. It proved the high point of the year. Though the fans took solace in winning their final game of the season, a 23–5 rout over Beaumont, the Sand Crabs' sixty-one wins and falling attendance disappointed Leopold. Financially strained, the merchant toyed with the idea of selling his franchise and found a buyer in local street contractor Walter A. Kelso. The new owner immediately took his $22,500 investment to Waco, and Galveston's three-decade history with the Texas League came to a sudden end.

3

POVERTY AND PROSPERITY

Grant County and Galveston

While Galveston admired its Texas League trophies, Grant County, Arkansas, received few awards. Arkansas lagged far behind Texas and most of the nation in terms of infrastructure and economic development. The state lacked access to a port other than those along the Mississippi River, and its transportation system remained primitive. Long-forgotten communities like Arkansas City and Helena loosely connected Arkansans with the economies of New Orleans and St. Louis. Massive floods and prolonged droughts made navigation along the Arkansas River unpredictable. Even the capital city, Little Rock, lacked many of the luxuries people elsewhere took for granted. Grant County families lived under far worse conditions.

Though timber brought limited prosperity to Grant County, and a rail line connecting Sheridan with Pine Bluff put an end to log drives along the Saline and Ouachita Rivers, the county's resources couldn't compete with the fertile soil of Arkansas' Delta. But poverty in the Delta was even more widespread. With sharecroppers beholden to large landowners and tenement farmers to their "company stores," a select few reaped the rewards of the region's agriculture.

Grant County's population remained steady through the end of the nineteenth century, the Sheridan–Pine Bluff rail line providing a ray of hope for its residents. As 1900 approached, hope for Grant County's future increased. The Sheridan Commercial Normal School paved the way for Missionary Baptist College, the first institution of higher education in the area. To many, increased population seemed a natural outgrowth.

Grant County's greatest claim to fame was and remains the Battle of Jenkin's Ferry during the Civil War. At Jenkin's Ferry, black Union soldiers atoned for the slaughter of surrendering black troops a few weeks earlier at Poison Spring. With the tables turned at Jenkin's Ferry, "Remember Poison Spring" became a rallying cry for the Union troops, who took no prisoners and their frustrations out on the same Confederate units who had slaughtered their fellow Northern soldiers. Other than Jenkin's Ferry, though, Grant County's claim to fame remained its timber, a plentiful resource in South Arkansas.

The lucrative cotton industry encouraged Grant County farmers to rely less on timber and try their hands at cultivating the cash crop. Though farmers found harvests small and difficult to transport to market, in the early 1900s, Grant County entered the cotton frenzy sweeping the South. Inexpensive land drew settlers from outside Arkansas, including Samuel Fausett, a farmer who had tilled ground in both Mississippi and his native Missouri.

Galveston's W.L Moody may have measured success in terms of business growth and financial assets, but Samuel Fausett's scale balanced on his family's survival from one winter to the next. In rural Arkansas, where almost everyone lived off the land, surviving meant having a large family capable of working a farm. Samuel's wife, Amanda Blanton Fausett, gave birth to eight children. Among the youngest, Robert Solon Fausett had moved from Missouri to Mississippi to Arkansas by age four, his family finally settling in the northeastern Grant County Township of Simpson in 1880. Just three years later, Samuel Fausett's death forced seven-year-old Robert to grow up quickly.

Farmers of South Arkansas' timber country suffered physical hardships regardless of age. Family farmers tamed the land with crude implements. Although the Delta offered soil better suited for cotton, independent farmers could make a better living elsewhere in Arkansas. Eventually, cotton became a cash crop in all seventy-five Arkansas counties. By the turn of the twentieth century, the Fausetts held their heads above water, a substantial accomplishment for an isolated family who had lived for seventeen years without the family patriarch.

In 1902, Robert Fausett set his sights on raising his own family. He married Mary Ella Ashley, recently returned to Grant County from Oklahoma. As the couple set to work on the Fausett farm, it's doubtful they even dreamed of the prosperity people experienced a world away along the Texas coast.

When Will Moody reached the age of nine, his parents sent him to boarding schools in his father's home state of Virginia. As a teenager, he enrolled in the Virginia Military Institute and eventually left the country for Europe. Returning to Texas a year later, Will briefly enrolled in the University of Texas Law School. Like his father, though, he didn't see a future in the profession. Will soon rejoined his father, now widely known as Colonel Moody, with his sights set on diversifying the family business interests.

Despite amassing considerable wealth, Colonel Moody taught his children to practice frugality and humility. Never one to flaunt his success or spend money on luxuries, Moody lived in two-story brick house near Twenty-third Street and M, a residence far less ornate than many Galveston antebellum homes. Even though the Colonel could easily afford to build each of his children a mansion, the family lived together for many years. A proven financial genius, Will took his father's conservative values and applied them to the cotton industry or, more precisely, expanding the family business beyond purchasing, processing and selling cotton as a commodity. Frugality and humility may have been fine virtues, but they didn't necessarily prohibit one from taking advantage of market factors to build wealth.

The W.L. Moody Sr. residence on Twenty-third Street, Galveston. *Courtesy of E. Douglas McLeod/Moody Archives.*

Will believed the cotton industry's real profit opportunities rested in credit and banking. Farmers needed loans to plant their crop and, upon harvest, would repay the funds with interest. If weather or other market factors left them unable to repay, the Moodys took title to whatever collateral the farmer provided or decided to float the grower for another season. Eventually, Will convinced his father of the profit potential and established W.L. Moody and Company (unincorporated). In 1889, he opened the private W.L. Moody and Company Bank, eventually merging with the National Bank of Galveston. With interests in both the cotton industry's mechanics and credit for growers, profits soared.

When the harbor-deepening project began, Galveston entered a period of unprecedented economic growth. Cotton industry leaders, dry goods merchants and manufacturers all converged on Strand Avenue. Immigrants from Europe arrived by the boatload, and Galveston's population soared, few having trouble finding work or success starting their own businesses.

Despite Will Moody's knack for finance, he did not live the "all work and no play" life recorded in many historical accounts. Both Moody and his father spent many hours hunting in Galveston and on the Bolivar Peninsula and fishing in Galveston Bay. Both hunted birds and ducks with the same passion with which they operated their company, and they often carried wealthy and elite visitors to favorite hunting spots. Presidential candidate William Jennings Bryan frequently hunted with the Moodys, his support of the gold standard and incentives to aid farmers earning their support. Politics, though, did not fit into the Moody aspirations, and Will felt far more at home sparring in the boxing ring. Most of all, though, the Moodys devoted themselves to family. In 1890, Will took the first step in shaping the next generation of Moodys when he married Libbie Rice Shearn, a member of another prominent Southeast Texas family.

After the two were married in Hull, Massachusetts, Will operated Moody interests in New York City. The younger Moody then decided to close the New York office, and the couple returned to Galveston, settling into a new home on Twenty-third Street, just west of Colonel Moody's. No doubt, his father's lessons in frugality had an impact on Will's choice

Opposite, top: The W.L. Moody Jr. residence at the corner of Twenty-third Street and M Avenue in Galveston. *Courtesy of E. Douglas McLeod/Moody Archives.*

Opposite, bottom: Shearn Moody (right) and his brother, William Moody III, in 1899. *Courtesy of E. Douglas McLeod/Moody Archives.*

of building materials, as he constructed a frame structure instead of brick. Regardless, Will Moody built a stately home anyone in Galveston would be proud to own.

Throughout the 1890s, Will continued to build his interests in banking and finance, all the while seeking other business pursuits. In the meantime, Libbie gave birth to their first child, Mary Elizabeth, in 1892. Within five years, the couple also had two sons, William Lewis Moody III and Shearn, as well as another daughter, Libbie. As the nineteenth century came to a close, Will and his father looked forward to continuing to build the fortunes of both the Moody name and Galveston, not only in Texas but also worldwide. Little did they know, those fortunes would soon face a test no other United States city had ever endured.

Though the Fausett family may have earned a meager living in Arkansas, by the end of 1900, they would be considered wealthy compared with many in Galveston.

4

ONE GREAT STORM, TWO NATURAL DISASTERS

By 1900, Galveston had firmly entrenched itself as the commercial center of Texas. Its improved wharves served as the port for shipping goods in and out of the growing state. Galveston led the nation in exports of cotton, cottonseed, hides, sugar, pecans and even cattle. In the first six months of 1900, 2.2 million bales of cotton left Galveston for textile mills in the Northeast and Great Britain. But while the city prospered as a port, it could not compete with nearby Houston in terms of manufacturing.

Houston's industrial businesses outnumbered those in Galveston by nearly 50 percent in 1900, with the mainland city's advantage surging. Throughout the 1890s, printing generated more revenue and provided more jobs than any industry in Galveston, outpacing flour milling by a three-to-one margin. Galveston officials publicly blamed the island's lack of industry on an inadequate supply of fresh water. City leaders recruited manufacturers by promoting Galveston's direct access to the Gulf of Mexico as a benefit over Houston, a city reached only via water on the difficult to navigate Buffalo Bayou. Still, Houston held advantages in terms of overland access, health and weather. Galveston's deep-water port allowed it to accommodate the largest cargo ships in the world, while railroads took advantage of Houston's proximity to the island. The potential for a lucrative civic partnership could not have been greater. But leaders of both cities knew that if Congress hadn't stepped in and assisted the Port of Galveston, Houston's economy would have grown much faster than its offshore neighbor's. Neither city did much to assist in aiding its rival's fortunes.

THE GALVESTON BUCCANEERS

In the late 1800s, yellow fever emerged as Galveston's greatest nemesis. At times, the disease reached epidemic proportions, placing the entire island under quarantine. Armed guards on the mainland prohibited people from disembarking boats or rail cars originating in Galveston, conjuring up memories of the Union blockade during the Civil War. Yet yellow fever represented only one of the health issues island residents faced. Diseases of all sorts ran rampant, a lack of suitable drainage filling the already saturated soil with animal and human waste to the point that pigs roamed freely to clean up the streets. Author Amelia Barr abandoned Galveston after losing several family members to disease, later labeling it as a "City of Dreadful Death" in her writings. Many islanders feared summer, and those with the means to leave the island during the humid months of July and August did so. For those left behind, mosquitoes made life a veritable hell. Will Moody left when business allowed, but each year he sent his family to summer in Virginia and Michigan.

In the fall of 1899, Libbie Moody informed Will that the family would remain together in future summers. The timing of her decision couldn't have been worse. A year later, Will, Libbie and the entire world learned that the Gulf of Mexico, not disease, posed Galveston's greatest threat.

The fact that Galveston lay in the path of many hurricanes was no secret. No fewer than ten hit the island during the nineteenth century, and many residents had seen and felt the impacts firsthand. Railroad financier Arthur Stillwell advised against investing too much money in rail service to Galveston, surmising that the infrastructure would be destroyed in short order. Likewise, other businesses shied away from the island's exposure to the Gulf of Mexico, and Houston reaped the rewards.

Though just a few miles inland, Houston was protected from the Gulf by the barrier islands and their tall sand dunes. But for the Moodys and thousands of others, the advantages of living in Galveston far outweighed the risks. Besides, expert geologists and meteorologists publicly deemed Galveston safe, its slowly sloping beach protecting the island from the most destructive of hurricane forces: the storm surge. Even though Galveston's highest point rested only a few feet above sea level, beachgoers observed large waves dissipating in the shallow waters on a regular basis. A hurricane's storm surge would surely meet a similar fate. Residents could mitigate high winds through improved construction standards, and they believed the brick buildings along Strand Avenue and the many homes in the city to be worthy opponents to the worst Mother Nature could offer. As the fall of 1900 approached, Galveston prepared for a new century of growth. With tourism a burgeoning industry, city leaders knew the Gulf of Mexico would play an important role in Galveston's future.

The first week of September 1900 seemed business as usual in Galveston. Harbor activity reached a frenzied pace as workers prepared cotton for shipping. The W.L. Moody Compress Company operated twenty-four hours a day, and its employees thrived on the extra income the season offered. Ship captains arriving in Galveston reported rough seas in the Gulf of Mexico, and local meteorologist Isaac Cline kept a close eye on reports that a major tropical storm had passed Cuba on a westward path. Even islanders aware of the storm showed little concern, though. Winds might damage a few buildings, which owners would quickly repair and return to routine business. This storm, however, would leave an indelible mark on Texas and United States history.

On September 8, a hurricane unlike any experienced brought torrential rains and rising tides to Galveston. When Will Moody heard the floodwaters below his third-story office on Strand tasted of salt, he realized this storm might be out of the ordinary. He sent Libbie word to evacuate the family to his father's brick home, expecting it to withstand the storm better than his frame house. Though Colonel Moody had traveled to New York on business, Libbie and the children waded through knee-deep water and climbed to his house's upper story. Over the next several hours, they watched a horrific scene unfold in the street below.

Accounts of the Moodys' experience during the 1900 hurricane are limited. Family members recall Mary Elizabeth, likely the only child old enough to remember the event in any detail, speak of houses, cows, pigs and people floating past them throughout the night. Most specifically, though, she recalled a particular playmate and her pet rabbits. A lifelong animal lover, Mary often stared into space as she recounted watching the raging sea carry her playmate's house down the street, followed by her rabbits and her family. She sorrowfully recalled never seeing the rabbits or her friend again.

When the storm finally moved inland and the Gulf of Mexico retreated, the tragedy in Galveston became clear. The "Great Storm of 1900" had reduced the wealthiest and most important city in Texas to rubble. Homes and businesses lay in waste, their owners' lifelong efforts swept from their foundations in a storm surge rushing across the island as if it didn't exist. But the physical wreckage told the least of the tale. As the days passed, the massive number of lives the storm swept from Galveston grew clear. Early estimates listed those lost in the hundreds, then over one thousand and eventually up to twelve thousand. The actual number killed will never be known, but most

Damage in Galveston, 1900. *Library of Congress.*

accounts place the loss at about six thousand, though Galveston's Rosenberg Library accepts seven to eight thousand as a better estimate. In a matter of hours, Galveston lost nearly one-fourth of its population to the same Gulf of Mexico that had built the city into a renowned port.

Though ultimately taking over a decade to complete, recovery from the storm began immediately. Colonel Moody's steamboat carried word to the mainland of the extent of destruction, and the Red Cross descended on the island as soon as transportation could be arranged. Relief committees consisting of prominent citizens quickly organized, with Will Moody appointed as treasurer of the donations arriving from around the world. The *Galveston Daily News*, certainly not spared from damage, didn't miss an issue, its September 9 edition a single page of names of those reported dead or missing. In the ensuing weeks, plumes of smoke arose across the island as workers burned enormous piles of debris. Even more agonizing was the stench of death that engulfed the island.

Galveston visitors roaming through its cemeteries today are often surprised at the few headstones dated September 1900. The reasons are disturbing but understandable. As people discovered bodies in the wreckage, they first brought them to a central location for possible identification. As time passed and the threat of disease grew, workers, some forced at gunpoint, hauled a majority

A body buried in Galveston's wreckage, 1900. *Library of Congress.*

of the bodies elsewhere on the island, where they burned thousands in great funeral pyres. Too many victims, too few workers and a rush to dispose of decaying bodies simply didn't allow for proper burials. Furthermore, looting of the most morbid kind became all too common. Searchers found many storm victims with fingers missing, those reaching the bodies first having cut them off, the victims too swollen for the lowest of Galveston's society to simply slip gold rings from their bodies. Some spoke of a man caught with a full sack of human fingers and gold. Reportedly, he was shot on the spot. Likewise, news reports claimed that many more people, mostly referred to as "negroes," were summarily executed under the martial law imposed on the city.

While Colonel Moody read reports of the Galveston destruction from New York, he questioned the true extent of the damage. Will sent word that the news reports did not exaggerate the situation and, in many cases, may have understated the impact. He also noted that many survivors vowed to leave the island permanently and rebuild their lives farther inland. Colonel Moody reportedly famously responded to his son that fewer people might be a good thing, after all. He noted, "We both like hunting, and the hunting will be all the better for us." Over the years, many interpreted his words to mean the Great Storm brought opportunities for profit. Yet the sentence isn't presented in context, and it's difficult to believe a man who spent thirty-five years helping build Galveston into a world-class shipping and commercial center would view the city's destruction and loss of workforce in a positive light. Furthermore, the written record of Colonel Moody's reaction to the storm tells a much different tale:

> Colonel W.L. Moody reached Galveston on Friday night...He had determined before he reached here that he would rebuild everything he had which had been damaged by the storm, and he was hoping that telegraphic communication would be restored so that the work of relieving the distress might be rendered more efficient.

When asked for a statement about his intentions, he said, in part:

> The people of this country have responded generously, liberally, to the cry for assistance; the disaster is appalling and appeals to the feelings and sympathies of mankind...Those who have suffered...will be cared for by a generous and sympathetic public.

On the future of Galveston, Moody noted that the city would be rebuilt "stronger and better than ever before":

> It was necessary to have a city here; that if the storm had swept the island bare of every human habitation and every structure...still men would come here and build a city...If I were in the accident insurance business I would rather insure a man against a storm in Galveston than a man in New York against accident on the railroads.

Finally, he pointed out how quickly the community responded to those in need and added that Texans exhibited confidence in the city. The Moody compress received bills of lading even after the storm's impact gained worldwide attention. The compress would be fully operational within a week.

Despite Moody's recorded statements, Texas legends can take on a life of their own, and those tied to the Great Storm of 1900 are many. In the publicity that followed, Colonel Moody's remark about hunting combined with events of early 1901 to paint a picture of the Moody family that many accepted as truth without knowing the facts. The Moody family motto evolved from "frugality and humility" to the more pointed, "Publicity only attracts two things: kidnappers and tax collectors." Perhaps "inaccurate information" should be third on the list.

In 1899, the wealthy widow Narcissa Willis lived with her housekeeper in a twenty-eight-thousand-square-foot mansion on the corner of

Broadway and Twenty-seventh Street. Shortly after leaving Galveston to visit her daughter, Beatrice Walthew, in New Jersey, Mrs. Willis passed away. Estranged from most of her family, the widow left a majority of her estate to Beatrice. No longer a Galveston resident and lacking any interest in returning, Beatrice placed the mansion on the auction block, accepting bids from the few able to afford a house valued at $200,000 (nearly $6 million in 2015). The estate was soon bogged down in legal challenges, and it wasn't until after the storm that the courts ruled Beatrice was legal owner of the mansion. By then, the imposing structure sat damaged, and the value of Galveston real estate had plunged.

Prior to the storm, Libbie Moody urged Will to bid on the thirty-one-room mansion. He placated his wife with a $20,000 bid, undoubtedly knowing he had no chance of competing with more motivated bidders. If Moody family values focused on frugality, humility and maintaining a low profile, owning an audacious mansion on a street called Broadway in Texas's most wealthy city did not fit the mantra.

Following the storm, with the future of Galveston and the extent of the mansion's damage unknown, bidders rapidly withdrew their offers.

W.L. Moody Jr. purchased the former Willis Mansion on Broadway in Galveston after the 1900 storm. *Courtesy of E. Douglas McLeod/Moody Archives.*

Beatrice still wanted to sell and contacted Will Moody, the sole remaining bidder, to inquire if his bid held firm. While he could have withdrawn his offer like other bidders, Moody remained true to his word, and in January 1901, he finalized the purchase. Had Moody known the extent of repairs necessary and the cost of modifying the enormous structure to accommodate plans to rebuild Galveston, he may not have been so anxious to please his wife. Nonetheless, Libbie got her wish, and the family soon moved into the mansion.

The facts of the mansion purchase fueled rumors that Will Moody took advantage of Beatrice Walthew by purchasing the massive home for "ten cents on the dollar." Moody detractors kept the legend alive, accusing the family of gaining wealth from others' misfortune. In reality, though, Will's purchase of the mansion at his original bid proved just the opposite. Moody was true to his employees, his community and, most importantly, his word.

Soon after the storm, Galveston residents realized returning the city to its previous splendor would not be completed in weeks, months or even years. Rebuilding the city's infrastructure could be done in short order, but Galveston had to rebuild its morale, convince businesses to return and overcome a worldwide reputation as a city on the brink of extinction. City leaders decided on the latter as the first step in a lengthy process.

Despite scientists' assurances of Galveston's immunity to storm surges, the entire world knew the fallacy of their theory. The island undoubtedly had experienced similar storm surges previously but not since recorded human occupation. Clearly, only drastic measures would allow Galveston to regain its status as a leading port. Over the next dozen years, the city endured a project the likes of which had never been attempted.

By 1902, U.S. Army and private engineers developed a plan to construct an eighteen-thousand-foot seawall along Galveston's beachfront. Designed to deflect the strength of waves from the Gulf, engineers set the seawall's elevation three feet above that of the 1900 storm surge. Experts expected the resulting engineering marvel to withstand a storm stronger than any living American had witnessed.

Financiers of the seawall included Galveston's elite and its working class. Civic pride stood tall as even children and the poorest residents donated the few dollars they could spare to the project. Galveston's entire population invested its money and heart into what many considered the most ambitious engineering project ever attempted. Voters then unanimously approved bonds and taxes to fundraising the city to seawall elevation, an effort requiring eleven million cubic yards of fill material. Virtually every structure in the city would be raised and streets turned into canals so massive amounts of sediment could be pumped from the sea. The physical remains of the 1900 storm would eventually be buried beneath up to seventeen feet of sand and silt. Unfortunately, the mental scars constantly rose to the surface.

During grade raising, Galveston became a "City on Stilts," with structures jacked high enough for fill material to be pumped beneath. Owners paid the cost of raising their buildings while the city provided fill material. Amazingly, not a single home or business owner disputed the expense. While the cost of raising Will Moody's Broadway mansion is unknown, over three hundred jacks lifted the huge structure the thirteen feet specified in the grading plan. Eventually, workers lifted over 2,100 homes, churches and businesses, along with streets, water and sewer lines and even graveyards. Galveston residents endured over a decade of inconvenience to save their city, and after the initial project, they continued to finance lengthening the seawall until it stretched over ten miles.

While raising the city seemingly offered defense against another devastating storm, the enormous amount of sediment dredged from Galveston Bay deepened the harbor even more than the twenty feet achieved years

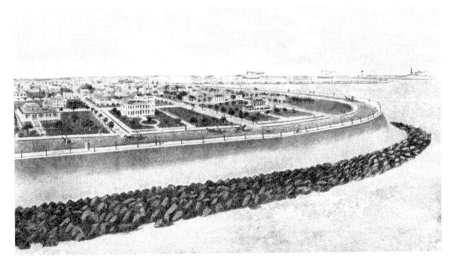

The Galveston Seawall is the island's most famous landmark and in the early 1900s was a magnificent feat of engineering. *Author's collection.*

earlier. Consistent, expensive dredging had maintained the depth, but the permanent removal of sediment placed the Port of Galveston in a class of its own. By the end of 1905, Galveston once again became the third-largest exporting port in the country, and seven years later, the city's wharves trailed only New York City in terms of activity.

With the bulk of the work completed and Galveston a strong commercial center, one question remained: would the seawall and grade raising actually protect the island against further storms? The answer came in 1915, when the most severe storm since 1900 struck the island. Despite eight deaths, some destruction and flooding of the island's lower elevations, the seawall and grade raising proved the engineering "marvel" its designers had touted. All along Seawall Boulevard, hotels remained open as violent waves crashed against the massive concrete wall standing between them and the sandbar the Gulf considered its prey. Modern ingenuity had indeed changed the fortunes of the beleaguered island.

While the engineering project progressed, Moody business ventures did not rest. In 1905, Will Moody expanded his interests into the insurance business his father mentioned in the storm's aftermath. Joining local business magnate Isaac Kempner, Moody established the American National Insurance Company (ANICO). Two years later, when the Robertson Law drove many other insurance companies from Texas, ANICO remained. When Moody bought Kempner's share of the business, ANICO grew into a powerful force in the insurance market. For his part, Kempner took his business

Shearn Moody, age twelve (1907). *Courtesy of E. Douglas McLeod/Moody Archives.*

William Moody III, W.L. Moody Jr. and Shearn Moody in their home's northern courtyard, 1908. *Courtesy of E. Douglas McLeod/Moody Archives.*

Shearn Moody (right) alongside his brother and father, 1910. *Courtesy of E. Douglas McLeod/Moody Archives.*

interests inland and made his fortune processing sugar cane, founding Ideal Sugar and the city of Sugarland in the process.

While family business interests experienced phenomenal success, Will and Libbie Moody also had to tend to children. In Moody tradition, Shearn and his brother moved to boarding schools for the majority of their teenage years. Will held hopes that his sons would return to Galveston with the same ambition and ideas for diversifying the W.L. Moody and Company's interests as he had in 1886. Ultimately, Shearn best met his father's expectations.

The average person standing in a cotton field wouldn't even notice a boll weevil. A quarter-inch-long beetle, an adult boll weevil arises during the spring, first appearing light yellow in color before slowly darkening to gray or black. Its long snout makes up nearly half its length, and throughout the summer, the boll weevil feasts on cotton buds, rapidly reproducing at the rate of ten generations a year. As a generation from a single female consists of three hundred offspring, the population increase over a decade is staggering and its impact unrivaled in American agricultural history.

A native of Central America, the boll weevil migrated northward during the 1800s, eventually reaching South Texas in 1892. Over the next eight years, the pest continued advancing slowly, and farmers and cotton buyers began to see the threat it posed to the economy. By 1900, boll weevils covered South Texas, and their destruction had an impact on cotton markets.

While the boll weevil needed little help in its migration, the Great Storm of 1900 almost instantaneously spread the pest throughout North and East Texas. The storm's furious winds carried boll weevils inland to areas several years beyond its reach under normal circumstances. The boll weevil's impact on the Texas cotton crop was immediate and severe. In 1904, the beetle infested much of East Texas and destroyed over 700,000 bales of cotton, an economic loss of over $40 million.

Soon, the boll weevil spread eastward, entering Louisiana and South Arkansas, states far less prepared to deal with a pest already proven virtually impossible to control. By 1908, the boll weevil had reached Central Arkansas' Grant County, where Robert and Mary Ella Fausett grew their farm and family. The same year, Mary Ella gave birth to the couple's youngest child, Robert Shaw Fausett. The youngster's time in Arkansas was short, but what he witnessed over the next eighteen years left a lifetime impression.

When the boll weevil entered North and East Texas, the Moodys and other industry leaders took notice. They pleaded for assistance to control a pest creating far more economic damage over a longer period than Galveston had suffered at the hands of the hurricane. Seamann Knapp, a New York native and Midwest agriculturalist, arrived in Texas to set up a demonstration farm in Terrell, east of Dallas. Over the next few years, Knapp developed methods of controlling the boll weevil that remain in use today. His success led Congress to establish the Cooperative Extension Service and signaled farmers east of Texas that the state was gaining the upper hand on the boll weevil. Sensing better opportunities in Texas, in 1911 Robert Fausett moved his family by covered wagon from Arkansas, ultimately settling in the Como-Pickton area of Hopkins County, just a few miles east of Sulphur Springs. Fausett operated a sizable farm in the area for decades, cotton its primary cash crop, with cattle and dairy also profitable. Robert reached a level of success his father had only dreamed about, but like Will Moody aspired to expand his father's already lucrative business, the youngest of the Fausett family also grew aspirations of his own.

Robert Fausett relied on the entire family to keep his farm profitable. Everyone pitched in, including his toddler son. As he grew, young Robert

Robert Fausett family (circa 1914). Buck Fausett is on the far left. *Courtesy of Robert J. Fausett.*

saw the toll farming took on his family, and he didn't like it. The boll weevil, still decades from being under any sense of "control," seemingly held the Fausett family hostage from spring through harvest each year. Some years they profited, and others they could barely repay creditors. Robert could not bear watching a tiny insect destroy a growing season's work, and he yearned for life away from the farm. In his spare time, he played sandlot baseball with nearby friends, his years in the fields building powerful arms and excellent hand-eye coordination. Soon, Robert took up football and other sports, excelling at all. Perhaps, he thought, he might have a means of escaping the unpredictable and mentally draining life of farming after all.

By the time Robert Fausett was born, Shearn Moody had survived the nation's worst recorded natural disaster and a bout with typhoid fever. Though he traveled extensively, Shearn's favorite pastimes included fishing and crabbing on family property along the San Luis Pass. Like his father and grandfather, Shearn loved hunting and fishing. But as with all Moody men, boarding school lay in Shearn's future. He first enrolled at Culver Military Academy in Indiana.

Military school and Shearn Moody created a perfect match, the young man's discipline making him a natural leader. At the same time, Shearn developed athletic prowess of his own. Though not tall and rather slender, he had grown into a stout young man. At Lawrenceville School in New Jersey, the sixteen-year-old became a noted athlete and member of the track and wrestling teams. Later, at the Evans School in Mesa, Arizona, he continued wrestling, a sport at which he

Shearn Moody, age sixteen, while attending Culver Military Academy. *Courtesy of E. Douglas McLeod/ Moody Archives.*

𝖣𝖆𝖛𝖎𝖘 𝖨𝖓𝖉𝗈𝗈𝗋 𝖳𝗋𝖆𝖼𝗄 𝖳𝖊𝖺𝗆, 1913

| RICHMOND | | STANLEY | MARTIN | | BLACK | MOODY |
| | KAUFFMANN | | JONES (CAPT.) | | ERDMAN | |

Shearn Moody at Lawrenceville (New Jersey) School, 1913. *Lawrenceville School Yearbook.*

excelled and which he enjoyed well into adulthood. Likewise, though not part a of an organized team, Shearn enjoyed baseball as much as any other boy his age, often playing outfield and catcher in pickup games between classes.

Upon Shearn's return from Arizona, Will Moody appointed him partner in City National Bank and vice-president of ANICO. While gaining his foothold as a businessman, though, the United States entered World War I, and like his grandfather who had formed a Confederate cavalry unit over a half century earlier, Shearn rushed to enlist in the army.

Patriotic young men in search of excitement find creative ways to enlist in the armed forces, whether by lying about their age, forging parental

Shearn Moody, in his navy uniform, alongside his father during World War I. *Courtesy of E. Douglas McLeod/Moody Archives.*

signatures or failing to release information disqualifying them from service. In filling out his military paperwork, Shearn Moody noted no physical impairments prohibiting him from serving. Whether he did so intentionally or mistakenly is unknown, but during training, the army deemed Shearn unfit for duty, his childhood bout with typhoid fever raising concerns that he might be a carrier of the disease. Though discharged and returned to

Galveston, Shearn remained determined to serve his country. He qualified for the Naval Reserve, remaining stateside to serve as a naval mapper and, ironically, a storm tracker. At war's end, he returned to ANICO full time. By 1920, the same year Colonel Moody died at the age of ninety-two, Shearn had shown his father the business sense required to someday manage the Moody financial interests.

Historians and even family members have described Shearn Moody as a hard-driving, hardheaded businessman. Bobby Moody Jr., born long after his grandfather's death, recalls family members speaking of Shearn as a "my way or the highway kind of guy." Yet accusations in historical accounts claiming Shearn was the "meanest, toughest, and tightest Moody of them all" with "the energy and personality of a fire hose" are likely overstated. Though it is doubtful anyone achieving Shearn's success could do so without a strong personality, family and newspaper accounts suggest Moody was a fun-loving and selfless soul dedicated to company employees and civic affairs.

In the early 1920s, Shearn starred in center field for the Kiwanis Club baseball team. While Sand Crabs fans suffered through another horrendous season, semipro and amateur baseball remained popular in Galveston. Civic- and company-league games received almost as much newspaper coverage as the Texas League franchise. As manager of the Kiwanis team in 1921, organization leaders publicly called Shearn to the carpet following a humiliating defeat at the hands of the rival Rotarians. As to why his teamed lost so badly, Shearn replied, "Two reasons. First, they had nine better players; second, the Rotarians team scored seven more runs." Such comments hardly seem as if they would come from a man with the personality of a fire hose.

Throughout the 1920s, Shearn remained involved in sporting activities on the island, often challenging Moody company employees to wrestling matches at outings and spending a great deal of time duck hunting. Much like his father and grandfather in the 1890s, Shearn hosted politicians and dignitaries on hunting excursions around Galveston. In January 1926, several prominent Houston residents, including the mayor, joined Shearn on an end-of-season duck hunt. The *Galveston Daily News*, Texas's oldest newspaper, which Shearn Moody purchased in 1923, noted any duck flying within three hundred yards of Moody's shotgun realized it had no chance at survival and simply gave up. Members of the hunting party undoubtedly expected great success with Moody as their guide.

With the hunting party aboard, Moody piloted the speedboat *ANICO* to a location near Lake Surprise on the bay side of Bolivar Peninsula. The *ANICO* stalled, and as those on board tried to restart the engine, the vessel

Shearn Moody and fellow Galveston resident Robert Lyons saved all but one of their hunting party's members when the speedboat *ANICO* exploded in 1926. *Courtesy of E. Douglas McLeod/Moody Archives.*

suddenly exploded. Six hunters jumped into the bone-chilling waters of East Bay to escape the flames.

Fire raged aboard the crippled vessel, but Shearn and Robert Lyons, a Galveston banker and hardware store owner, remained aboard, tossing life preservers to those in the water. Eventually, the fire consumed the entire boat, forcing both into the water as well. After two hours, a rescue party finally arrived; however, it was too late for Houston attorney E.R. Warkin, who died from exposure. The remainder suffered a few burns, broken ribs and various degrees of hypothermia. But without the heroic efforts of Shearn Moody and Robert Lyons, it's unlikely any would have survived.

Arriving at the Galveston wharves a few hours later, Shearn saw his fellow hunters off in ambulances but refused transport to the hospital for himself. Instead, he returned to his Broadway home and spoke little of the incident or his courageous efforts. After all, publicity attracted only kidnappers and tax collectors. Shearn Moody chose to remain humble and silent, though he could have easily been lauded as a hero.

In the late 1920s, Shearn became the entrepreneur his father had hoped he would. He held senior roles in a variety of new ventures, including the National Fire Insurance Company, the Texas National Fire Insurance

Company, General Crude Oil Company, Rex Steam Laundry and the Galveston Block Company. He also realized Galveston had fallen short of its potential as a tourist destination. Shearn Moody intended to lead the way in building the island's tourism industry.

While Shearn Moody busily expanded family business interests and played the role of quiet hero in Galveston, 250 miles north, Robert Fausett searched for an escape from farming. At age seventeen, Robert had seen enough cows, chickens and failed cotton crops to last a lifetime, and spending his afternoons at the Como-Pickton General Store no longer satisfied his sense of adventure. Robert had grown into an imposing figure, particularly anywhere a pickup game of baseball might spring up. Although just five feet, ten inches tall and 170 pounds, Robert had built strength from his life on the farm. He knew he stood at a crossroads. Unless he finished high school, few opportunities lay beyond the boundaries of Hopkins County. He could either surrender to pursuing a life he despised or find something better. "Better" lay just 30 miles northwest in Hunt County.

Commerce, Texas, sprang from the prairie in 1872, in short order becoming a commercial center. By 1894, the nearby East Texas Normal College had moved to Commerce, offering higher education in a community never growing beyond a few thousand residents. By 1917, the State of Texas had acquired the school, renaming it East Texas Teachers College (ETTC), its mission to educate teachers to work in rural school districts.

ETTC provided a training school or "sub-college" for those having finished tenth grade. Not only did the training school grant high school diplomas, but it also provided real-world teaching experiences for ETTC students. The chance to complete high school lured Robert Fausett to Commerce, but the opportunity to play organized sports held just as much appeal. ETTC fielded teams in track, football, baseball and other athletic activities, with the training school a sort of junior varsity program. While ETTC proudly sported the "Lions" mascot for its athletic programs, the "Cubs" represented the training school. When Fausett arrived on campus, coaches quickly realized they had found a Lion.

Fausett played for the varsity Lions football team his first semester, but his performance must have been unimpressive. His name appears in no newspaper articles covering the season; in fact, the only mention of Fausett

Upon entering the East Texas Teachers College training school, Buck Fausett initially played sports on the Cubs teams, a junior varsity version of the college's Lions athletic teams. *Courtesy of Robert J. Fausett.*

is below the team photo published in *The Locust* yearbook. When it came to baseball, though, no one could overlook Fausett's presence.

During his two years in Commerce, "Leaky" Fausett, as he was called, played shortstop and pitcher. While "Leaky" might have been an apt nickname for a fellow named Fausett, Robert certainly wasn't leaky when it came to his play on the diamond. An outstanding fielder and power hitter, he led the Lions through a schedule against local amateur teams, high schools and conference opponents, including Stephen F. Austin, Daniel Baker College and Sam Houston State. In 1928, he helped the Lions to a 12-2 record, outscoring their opponents 131–66 and claiming the Texas Interscholastic Athletic Association championship. He remained at ETTC through 1929, with yearbook captions noting him pitching the Lions to victory and regularly slamming home runs out of the park.

Upon graduating, Fausett played amateur ball in Fort Worth before briefly returning to his native Arkansas to play professionally with Pine Bluff of the Cotton States League. In 1931, he signed with the Longview Cannibals of

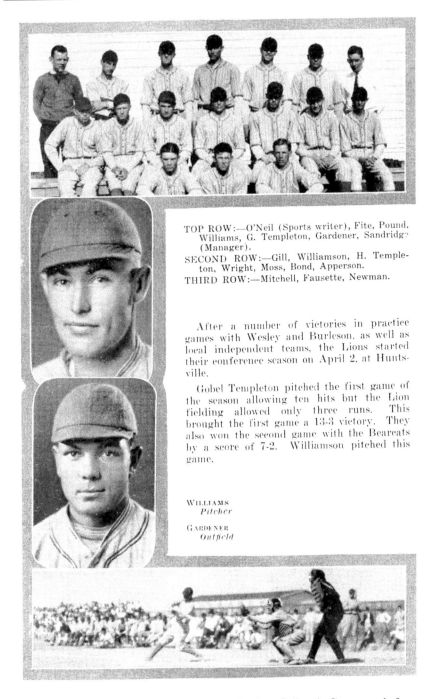

TOP ROW:—O'Neil (Sports writer), Fite, Pound, Williams, G. Templeton, Gardener, Sandridge (Manager).
SECOND ROW:—Gill, Williamson, H. Templeton, Wright, Moss, Bond, Apperson.
THIRD ROW:—Mitchell, Fausette, Newman.

After a number of victories in practice games with Wesley and Burleson, as well as local independent teams, the Lions started their conference season on April 2, at Huntsville.

Gobel Templeton pitched the first game of the season allowing ten hits but the Lion fielding allowed only three runs. This brought the first game a 13-3 victory. They also won the second game with the Bearcats by a score of 7-2. Williamson pitched this game.

WILLIAMS
Pitcher

GARDENER
Outfield

Buck Fausett played two seasons at East Texas Teachers College in Commerce before turning professional. *Courtesy of Texas A&M University–Commerce Special Collections.*

the East Texas League, but both the team and league folded after only two weeks. At age twenty-three, Fausett became a ballplayer without a team, and he didn't consider returning to the family farm an option. Fortunately, he made a name for himself on the sandlot diamonds of Fort Worth and during his brief professional stints in Pine Bluff and Longview. Word spread to Galveston of a youngster with a bright future in baseball, and Shearn Moody wasted little time in signing him to a team that had just made a triumphant return after a six-year hiatus from the Texas League.

No discussion of Galveston recreation would be complete without mentioning the era of Prohibition, the Maceo family and a period in which the island earned its nickname "The Free State of Galveston."

Salvatore and Rosario Maceo immigrated to Louisiana from Italy in 1901. They moved to Galveston before World War I and opened a barbershop that met limited success for several years. With the Eighteenth Amendment's passage in 1919, the manufacture, sale and consumption of alcohol in the United States became illegal. The Maceo brothers began presenting their customers with Christmas gifts of homemade wine made from old family recipes. Beginning innocently enough, the wine soon built the Maceo barbershop into a thriving business. When Rosario earned over $1,000 in a single weekend storing a load of smuggled liquor under his house, the Maceo brothers realized the potential profits Prohibition offered. In the coming years, they set up a vice-oriented empire in Galveston, with liquor, gambling and prostitution as its backbone. The Maceos, just as much a mob as those ruling the Chicago underworld, thrived in Galveston, Sam's sparkling personality and generosity making him a friend of many on the island. As the operation grew and local law enforcement turned a blind eye to the Maceo syndicate, tourists flocked to Galveston. Maceo-run businesses also attracted many conventions to the island, including the state police and other law enforcement organizations, their members taking advantage of the after-hours recreational opportunities.

With firmly held religious beliefs, the Moodys opposed gambling, drinking, smoking and most every other activity of questionable moral character. But Will and Shearn recognized the Maceo influence on the island as too strong to overcome. Rather than fight it, they decided to use it to their advantage. While Galveston offered plenty of "speakeasies" and hosted well-known

The Buccaneer Hotel offered Galveston's most luxurious accommodations and served as the scene of several Galveston Buccaneers celebrations. *Author's collection.*

establishments like the Balinese Ballroom and the Hollywood Club, the island sorely lacked visitor accommodations. In 1927, Shearn Moody led his company's plunge into the hotel business, overseeing construction of the Jean Lafitte Hotel. Soon after, he built the Buccaneer on Seawall Boulevard and acquired one of Galveston's oldest hotels, the Galvez. The hotels thrived right along with the Maceo syndicate, but the crime family didn't attempt to place slot machines in Moody-owned facilities. Sam knew they would not be welcomed.

Written records suggest the Moodys and Maceos had no relationship beyond that of businessmen seeking to develop Galveston into a prosperous city, for both their fellow citizens and personal commercial interests. The Maceos built their fortune illegally but with overwhelming support of island residents and a police force disinterested in enforcing federal laws. It seemed everyone in Galveston had at least one relative or close friend employed by the Maceos, and even as the country entered the Great Depression, the Galveston economy remained robust. Visitors flocked to the seemingly lawless island off the Texas coast. Eventually, Shearn Moody expanded the family's holdings and formed the National Hotel Company. Though the Moodys didn't approve of the Maceos, they tolerated the family's misgivings, as they kept Galveston's citizens employed and business prosperous.

Galveston historians generally agree that Sam Maceo and Will Moody met at least once after the Buccaneer Hotel's opening. Moody caught wind of Maceo's plans to capitalize on the hotel business and summoned Sam to a meeting in his office. Will told Maceo in no uncertain terms that the Moodys did not engage in gambling, and he expected the Maceos to stay out of Galveston's hotel industry. Reportedly, the two exchanged few words but left with an understanding. Within hours, bulldozers destroyed the foundation of a hotel Sam Maceo had planned to construct.

While Galveston's hotels lured the rich and famous, Shearn Moody didn't ignore less wealthy visitors who came to enjoy the beach and carnival-like tourist attractions popping up along the seawall. In 1928, he constructed Miramar Courts, a low-budget tourist court on Seawall Boulevard between Thirty-third and Thirty-fifth Streets. A one-stop shop for vacationers, Miramar Courts offered a grocery store, a pharmacy and a full-service garage with gasoline, as well as one of the first miniature golf courses in the nation.

Shearn Moody believed Galveston had the "something" needed to succeed as a tourist destination, with glamour, atmosphere and a historical tradition making the island far more than a playground. The *Galveston Tribune*, a newspaper Moody purchased and combined with the *Daily News* in 1926, described Shearn as an "unqualified optimist with respect to the great development awaiting the city and Port of Galveston," development it claimed would maintain community and civic heritage. By 1930, Shearn Moody had reached out to reclaim an important part of that heritage: professional baseball.

5
A TAXING RETURN

When Nelson Leopold sold the Sand Crabs to W.A. Kelso after the 1924 season, he claimed he really hadn't intended to do so. He placed them on the auction block as an experiment and was surprised when the local contractor offered a more than fair price. Over the ensuing years, Waco officials sold Leopold's players to other teams and generated a profit of $65,000, leaving Leopold second-guessing his decision. Regardless, Kelso soon left the Texas League as well, selling his club to Waco stockholders. For the next six seasons, Galveston remained without professional baseball, with semipro and amateur leagues filling the void.

In 1929, Shearn Moody privately set his sights on bringing Texas League baseball back to Galveston. The island attracted tourists, and locals turned out nightly for games between teams sponsored by the Galveston Wharf Company, Dr. Pepper Bottling and Galveston Dairy. In February, the Galveston Amateur Baseball Federation elected Moody president, and he acknowledged his goal to bring professional baseball back to the city. But, he added, the city lacked a stadium built to professional standards. Moody appointed a commission to consider vacant areas where a stadium might be constructed. When the Galveston Amateur Baseball Association began play at School Park in March, one thousand fans looked on as the mayor showed support for Moody's efforts, throwing the season's first pitch with Shearn as catcher.

Throughout 1929, Galveston liberals fought hard against Moody interests, claiming Shearn was in talks with Democrats to elect him mayor.

In such a case, opponents claimed, the city commission would become one of Moody's hired hands. Their fears never materialized, and Moody never ran for political office. He focused on the one issue at hand: returning professional baseball to Galveston. The entire city would reap the economic benefits of Class A ball, as fans would patronize local businesses, including Maceo clubs and Moody hotels. Professional baseball seemed a winning proposition for Galveston, and Moody quietly held talks with Texas League officials throughout the 1930 season.

In early January 1931, Shearn announced his intention of having a Texas League club in Galveston by the start of the season, only three months away. But, he said, he would be unsuccessful without local support. While Moody's financial backing would certainly help the effort, fans needed to show interest in a team. Financial difficulties plagued Waco and Shreveport's franchises, and Moody confidently promoted a united effort to relocate one of them to Galveston. He recommended a stock company franchise and improved streetcar service to a new lighted ballpark. After all, Galveston thrived on its nightlife, and baseball under the lights would only enhance it.

While Moody built local support for a ball club, he also lobbied Texas League officials. League president J. Alvin Gardner, a former batboy for the Beaumont club and semipro ballplayer, encouraged owners to seriously consider placing a franchise in Galveston. The Dallas oil contractor recognized the value in reviving the Galveston-Beaumont-Houston rivalry and the financial savings in grouping the southern clubs as tightly as possible. Gardner noted Galveston as an ideal amusement center where night baseball would appeal to the working class. In fact, he assured other owners that Galveston would be a far better location for night baseball than Waco. Gardner's words sealed the deal. Within days, Shearn Moody entered negotiations with Waco officials and visited Exporter Park in Beaumont, considered the finest stadium in Texas.

Victor Emanuel, sports editor for the *GDN*, erroneously wrote that Moody was no great fan of the game but a businessman who understood the value of a Texas League franchise in the city. The respected sportswriter's words fueled Moody's efforts, and he offered $23,500 for the Waco club. He also one-upped the city in its plans to upgrade School Park by planning a completely new stadium modeled after Exporter Park on ten acres of vacant land along Winnie Avenue between Fifty-first and Fifty-third Streets. For its part, the City of Galveston agreed to improve access to the area by shelling parking lots and installing sidewalks from streetcar stops.

Waco barely resisted Moody's effort to reacquire what had once been Galveston's franchise. The Cubs profited only about $2,000 a year, all of it coming from selling players. But when Waco could afford only the least-skilled players, even those profits dried up. The Cubs $70,000 annual expenses fell far behind the rest of the Texas League, where owners normally spent between $100,000 and $150,000 on their franchises each year. Backed by a groundswell of support from Galveston, J. Alvin Gardner and other Texas League team owners, Moody had a deal within a week. He announced plans for a ballpark constructed of steel, concrete and cypress, with seating in the northwest corner of the site to provide constant shade for afternoon games. The stadium would offer box, reserved, grandstand and bleacher seating, and Moody assured Galveston's African American fans that their segregated seating area would have the same first-class accommodations.

"The island needs Class A baseball," Moody stated. Thanks to his quick efforts and the support of the Galveston Booster Club in promoting stock sales among local investors, Galveston would have professional baseball back in time for the spring opener.

Sportswriter Victor Emanuel pressured fans to support their club even though it would not likely compete for the pennant and predicted Del Pratt, manager of the Waco franchise for its entire existence, would build a winner in Galveston within four seasons. He assured fans that Pratt would bring thirty-five quality players to Galveston for training and commended Moody for addressing an issue of great civic importance. Since the team had left town six seasons before, Galveston had become a city with many visitors and attractions. Moody's club would surely be successful, Emanuel wrote, also noting the baseball team would provide much-needed jobs. Though Moody asked Emanuel and other writers to choose the team's name, they deferred to the fans, offering a season ticket to the person providing the best suggestion. The most popular submissions included the Sand Crabs, Breezers and Buccaneers.

Within two weeks of setting his sights on the Waco franchise, Shearn Moody managed to purchase the team, design a stadium, sell season tickets and attract an early February Texas League meeting to the Buccaneer Hotel. His large ballpark would have left and right field walls 350 feet from home plate, with dead center a distance of 450 feet. The spacious outfield, along with the heavy sea air, would reduce the cost of lost baseballs, as fewer home runs and more foul balls would remain in the park.

After impressing fellow franchise owners at the February meeting, Moody said the ballpark's lighting would provide 200,000-foot candles over the playing field, making night baseball every bit as bright as afternoon games. Victor Emanuel continued to laud Moody's accomplishments, and when designers increased the center field distance to 461 feet, he predicted plenty of offense and exciting inside-the-park home runs. Finally, he recommended the stadium be named "Moody Field" in honor of Shearn, who also happened to be Emanuel's boss. Ultimately, "Moody Stadium" won out.

The Moody name stirred excitement throughout professional baseball. Commissioner Kennesaw Mountain Landis, famous for his handling of the Chicago Black Sox scandal of 1919, planned to attend opening day on April 29, when the Galveston Buccaneers, named in honor of the island's pirate heritage and the Moody hotel, would host the Beaumont Exporters.

While league and city officials eagerly awaited opening day, few showed more excitement than Galveston's schoolboys. Most had never seen professional baseball and became mesmerized as the stadium grew from the vacant lot. In a special effort to include Galveston's youth, Shearn Moody formed the Buccaneer "Knothole Gang," a club of boys and girls of all races who could attend weekday games at no charge. Lifelong Galveston resident Stanford Elbert, an eleven-year-old, rushed to join.

"Moody was a very stern man," Elbert recalls. "We got a free ticket and a 'soda water,' but in return we had to agree to a lot of rules."

Indeed, Knothole Gang members swore to a code of ethics. Anyone under the age of fifteen could join, but Moody provided ground rules for their continued membership. No Knothole Gang member would be allowed to skip school to attend a game, attend without his or her parents' permission or throw anything in the stands or onto the field. All members would make every effort to attend church, would practice clean speech and habits and would not be allowed into games on Sundays or holidays.

Stan Elbert fondly remembers his days as a member of the Knothole Gang.

"The players were all very gentlemanly," he said. "They treated all of us kids well and offered autographs and souvenirs."

When asked if future letters to the editor of the *GDN* complaining of the group's antics in shouting down umpires and tossing rotten fruit in their direction had merit, Elbert adamantly denied anything of the sort.

"Moody would have never stood for it," he said. "We were on our best behavior at all times."

Unfortunately, the 1931 Buccaneers couldn't live up to Moody's standards on the ball field.

———•———

When Del Pratt brought his Waco club to Galveston, sportswriter Vic Emanuel gushed over the team to the point that his excitement outweighed his sports sense. Since assuming management of the Cubs for the 1925 season, Pratt had led the team to a winning record only once, repeatedly finishing in the bottom half of the Texas League standings. Still, when it came to Texas League managers of the 1920s, few are as well remembered as Derrill Burnham Pratt.

Pratt was born in 1888, a native of Walhalia, South Carolina. His father, George Pratt, was well known in the South Carolina cotton industry. By 1902, the Pratt family had relocated to Alabama, where George managed a cottonseed company and ultimately became a cotton broker. While George Pratt didn't acquire Moody-like wealth, his family led privileged lives, and when Del graduated high school, his parents could easily afford to send him to college. He began studying at what would eventually become Auburn University before transferring to the University of Alabama in 1908.

At Alabama, Pratt lettered in both football and baseball while working toward a degree in textile engineering. As shortstop for the baseball team, he served as team captain and led it to the 1909 conference championship when Alabama posted a 19-3 won-loss record. Following graduation, Del enrolled in law school but soon gave it up for professional baseball. His career began in Montgomery, Alabama, but after only one season, he joined the St. Louis Browns. In the meantime, Pratt spent the off-season coaching college sports, including both football and baseball. From an early age, Del exhibited leadership skills and management abilities that even more experienced coaches lacked.

While in St. Louis, Del Pratt had a memorable five-year streak in which he played in every game with the exception of one—he was suspended for the second game of a double-header after arguing with the umpire in the first. Had it not been for the ejection, Pratt would have played in well over seven hundred consecutive games. Not surprisingly, Pratt became best known for consistency. He ranked among major-league leaders in games

Del Pratt managed the Waco/Galveston franchise from 1925 to 1932, posting only one winning season. *Library of Congress, Prints & Photographs Division, LC-DIG-ggbain-13885.*

played, batting average, hits, extra-base hits and RBIs through the 1917 season. Switching from his college position of shortstop to second base, Del initially struggled as a fielder, but after a few seasons, the *Sporting News* named him the best second baseman in the majors.

Pratt did not shy from controversy. He and a teammate filed a $50,000 libel suit against Browns owner Phil Ball who called them out for not giving full effort on the field. Years later, a member of the 1919 Chicago "Black Sox" added fuel to the fire, accusing the Browns of intentionally dropping a double-header. Pratt and his teammate won their suit but received far less compensation than they hoped.

After playing briefly with the crosstown Cardinals, the New York Yankees acquired Pratt in 1918. In the coming three seasons, he remained consistent, missing only one game at second base. But even then, he couldn't escape controversy. He initially refused to play for the Yankees without a pay increase. Then, after the team finished in third place, Pratt protested bonuses paid to team employees of shares paid to the players who had earned them. He and a few teammates threatened to strike over the affair, but the Yankees eventually satisfied them by paying each player an additional thirty-seven dollars. Soon, Pratt had plenty more to complain about, as the Yankees traded him to the Red Sox just after the famous Babe Ruth transaction between the two teams. Pratt played for a lowly Boston club for two years while moonlighting as a coach in the college ranks. In 1922, the Red Sox traded him to Detroit, where he played three more seasons, continuing to bat over .300. But age eventually caught up with Del, and by the end of 1924, the majors had little use for the durable second baseman. For the next few months, he managed a sporting goods store in Michigan.

When the Waco Cubs called on Pratt to manage their new franchise in 1925, he one-upped them on the offer. Not only would he manage the team, but he would save the owner money by playing as well. Over the next several seasons, Pratt batted as well as he ever had in the majors, increasing his power and posting lofty numbers. In 1927, the thirty-nine-year-old won the Texas League Triple Crown, batting .386 with thirty-two home runs and 140 RBIs. Pratt slowed in ensuing seasons, playing mostly as a first baseman and reducing his at-bats. Still, he never fully gave up as a player-manager, and when Shearn Moody retained him when the Cubs moved to Galveston, Moody had little doubt he would be getting two for the price of one, a financial deal any Moody would have recognized as a net gain.

All of Galveston greeted opening day in 1931 as a rebirth of sorts. Professional baseball had returned to the city, and once again, Galveston appeared in statewide sports pages. Shearn Moody hosted a gala grand opening at Moody Stadium on April 29. As promised, baseball commissioner Kennesaw Mountain Landis attended, along with a host of dignitaries. Many heralded the stadium as the finest in minor-league baseball, Moody's wise judgment in placing the park on the bay side of the island no small factor. The ballpark attracted streams of Galveston fans and visitors, but the 1931 Buccaneers didn't put on nearly as impressive a performance on the ball field as management did for Moody Stadium's grand opening.

Despite Victor Emanuel's daily gushing in his sports column, Del Pratt didn't bring a very good ball club to Galveston, and the Waco Cubs' habit of

A crowd of dignitaries gathered in Moody Stadium for its grand opening in 1931. The Knothole Gang appears in the grandstands. *Courtesy Tom Kayser/Texas League.*

finishing near the bottom of the standings followed them to Moody Stadium. Though he signed some heavy hitters in Texas A&M standout Roy "Beau" Bell, Harvey Belieu and Larman Cox, even at age forty-three Pratt inserted himself into half of the Buccaneers' games. Throughout the season, he constantly shifted the lineup, with no fewer than thirty-nine players appearing on the roster. Only four fielders played a half season, and outfielders Cox and Bell led the team with .276 and .273 batting averages, respectively.

The 1931 Galveston Buccaneers committed over 225 errors, led by shortstop Keith Molesworth's 62. Molesworth booted the ball on nearly one of every ten attempts, but his .272 batting average kept him in the lineup for 161 games. Every fielder Del Pratt placed in the lineup manufactured errors faster than the Moody compress could bale cotton. The poor fielding may have helped keep Buccaneers pitchers' ERAs in an acceptable range, but it did not help their win-loss records.

Former Cincinnati Reds pitcher Bill Harris tied with Preacher Thurman at eleven wins, but Harris's twenty-one losses overshadowed a respectable 2.87 earned run average. Behind Harris and Thurman, Del Pratt's roster had little pitching talent. Two future major leaguers, Andy Bednar and Ed Carrol, combined for just eight wins against twenty-three losses. Despite pitching 183 innings on the season, Marty Dernovich finished with a 1-13 record. Henry Thormahlen contributed another nineteen losses. Of the fifteen pitchers Del Pratt used in 1931, seven pitched over 100 innings, but just one, Russell Cromer, posted a winning record. The disastrous season left the Buccaneers with a 57-104 record, the worst in the city's long professional baseball history. After remaining buried in last place the entire season, Pratt and Shearn Moody vowed to return better and stronger in 1932.

While Shearn Moody wanted a winner on the field, he also wanted to place the Texas League on notice that Galveston had reentered the league, and any other team expecting to compete with the Buccaneers at the gate faced stiff competition. Moody emphasized off-season tickets sales, enlisting the help of local charities in competition for a cash prize. He announced his intention to win the Attendance Cup presented to the team drawing the most fans for its home opener. Considering he would be competing against larger cities like Dallas, Fort Worth and Houston, Moody placed the burden squarely on Buccaneers fans to bring the trophy to Galveston.

As the 1932 season approached, the Texas League and all of baseball grappled with the issue of radio. Live game broadcasts fueled public interest and allowed loyal fans to follow their team when they couldn't make it to the ballpark. Yet a veteran baseball man like Del Pratt remained staunchly opposed.

"When a man can sit at home, light a cigar, and pull off his coat and shoes, and twirl the knob to tune in a good baseball game," Pratt said, "he would too often be content to stay away from the ballpark." Moody backed his manager, and Galveston joined other Texas League teams in prohibiting broadcasts.

By February, Del Pratt anxiously awaited to reconvene his team. The previous season reflected poorly on his reputation, and Pratt held rookie tryouts at Moody Field early in the year in hopes of discovering an unknown prize. Although signing two candidates from the tryouts, neither made the roster.

League president J. Alvin Gardner recognized Galveston's lack of an agreement with a major-league franchise or a lower-level minor-league affiliate hindered its ability to build a winner. He used the Bucs' situation to lobby for a Class D league in Texas, receiving both his wish and a second job when the new Dixie League asked him to serve as its president as well. Gardner did note in early March that he had seen a vastly improved Buccaneer lineup. With Bill McGehee, Gene "Half-Pint" Rye and pitcher George Darrow, he anticipated the Bucs would compete for the pennant in 1932. Based on the season's outcome, it's likely he exaggerated the talent pool to increase fan interest statewide.

Del Pratt wasted little time backing up Gardner's claims, confidently naming Art Seydler and his 8-6 record of 1931 the "vanguard of 1932." Likewise, he boasted Ed Carroll had more "stuff" than any pitcher in Texas and touted the acquisition of Frank Tubbs and his two career no-hitters. Unfortunately, Carroll's "stuff" had earned him a 2-12 record the year before, and Tubbs's best years appeared well behind him. But after lauding Beau Bell as the most improved player on the team, Pratt rethought his assessment. "We are an 'If' team," he stated. "If we get off on the right foot, no Depression will be felt in this city."

One addition to the 1932 Bucs roster went largely unnoticed. Robert Fausett, after a short 1931 stint with Beaumont, signed as a utility infielder for the Bucs. For Fausett, the Texas League was a far cry from Fort Worth's sandlots, and he set out to make the best of his opportunity. His "utility" label did not last long. Fausett cracked the starting lineup at third base early in the season.

Despite the dramatically different childhoods of Buck Fausett and Shearn Moody, fate seemed to bring the two together in Galveston. Although Moody came from a life of privilege and Buck from a hardworking farm family, both had determination. Shearn Moody set his sights on a business goal and didn't rest until he achieved it. Buck Fausett set an escape from the farm as his goal, and when he finally managed to get away, he never looked back. But the destiny bringing the two together had been set in motion eight years before Buck was even born. The same storm four-year-old Shearn Moody had watched destroy Galveston helped pushed the boll weevil into Arkansas the year of Buck's birth. And the tiny insect's destructive wake ultimately drove Buck Fausett from the farm to pursue a baseball career, landing him at Shearn Moody's desk signing a contract with the Buccaneers.

Had Fausett not shed the nickname "Leaky" while playing with Longview in early 1931, he may have never made it to Galveston. Nicknames could be larger than life in Depression-era baseball, and "Leaky" would hardly draw the attention of a team already prone to errors. But in his two weeks at Longview, Fausett rifled throws across the diamond from third base. As the Cannibal first baseman felt the ball pop in his mitt, he'd throw it to the ground, shaking the sting from his hand. "Lay off the buckshot, fella!" he shouted. Teammates shortened "Buckshot" to "Buck," and it remained the name Fausett carried through his career.

The latest snowfall in Galveston history interrupted spring training in March, and perhaps Shearn Moody and Del Pratt should have taken it as a sign of things to come. Pratt used the few days off to cut promising young infielder Charlie English, perhaps the one player who might have warmed what turned out to be a rather cold Buccaneers lineup.

Galveston did improve slightly in 1932, but the same problems as the previous season ailed them. Fielding remained miserable, with shortstop Keith Molesworth's fifty-four errors adding to a ballooning career total. Buck Fausett added thirty-seven of his own, and for the second consecutive season, the Bucs committed over two hundred errors. Unlike 1931, though, improved batting occasionally helped the pitching staff weather the storm. Henry Thormahlen's twenty wins led the team, with George Darrow posting fifteen of his own. Del Pratt's "vanguard" Art Seydler ended the year with a 7-13 record and 3.80 ERA, while George Tubbs pitched only sixty-six innings with a 1-7 record.

Like the previous season, over thirty players appeared on the Bucs' 1932 roster, but this time ten played in at least 124 games. Former major leaguer Gene Rye anchored a formidable outfield, bringing power and a .306 batting average to Galveston, statistics bolstered by Beau Bell and Larman Cox's steady bats. Carl Frey platooned successfully, but a virtually unknown arrived in Galveston early in the season eventually developed the Buccaneers' outfield into the league's best.

Left-handed batter Antone "Tony" Governor was born in Clarksburg, California, in 1903. Though playing briefly in 1920 in the Pacific Coast League, Tony didn't make another professional appearance until four years later, when he signed with Oakland, eventually batting .274 in consecutive seasons. Though lacking power, Governor's speed helped him turn would-be ground outs into infield singles and singles into extra-base hits. In 1931, Governor played in the "Three-I" League, batting .326 before finishing the season with Little Rock of the Southern Association. He moved farther south in 1932, beginning the year at Beaumont before signing with Galveston. In just 128 games, Governor pounded out 160 hits, including 44 for extra bases, while posting a team leading .319 average. His 217 total bases ranked third for the team, despite the fact that he appeared in 22 fewer games than leader Larman Cox, who bested Governor by only 19 bases.

Tony Governor, 1934 outfielder. *Courtesy of Rosenberg Library, Galveston, Texas.*

Del Pratt inserted himself into the 1932 lineup fifteen times, batting a highly respectable .293 for a forty-four-year-old skipper who had been involved in professional baseball since 1910. Though the Bucs showed slight improvement in the standings over the previous season, most of the headlines from Galveston in 1932 related to chaos involving league rules. At the prodding of Del Pratt, Shearn Moody kept ardent supporter J. Alvin Gardner busy all season long.

Though automobiles and buses had gained in popularity, Texas League teams stuck with railroads for transportation. Players could set their watches by railroad schedules, but bus travel had yet to become reliable. As night games gained popularity, catching the evening's last railroad connection in time to arrive in another city the following day became vital. Texas League rules declared a game official after five innings, and owners adopted a rule allowing a team to leave one hour before its train departed if an official game had been played. Several controversies arose over the rule, and Shearn Moody became personally involved in more than one.

On July 13 in Galveston, San Antonio manager Homer Hammond refused to continue playing a game beyond 10:00 p.m., citing that his team had to catch an 11:00 p.m. train. The game remained a half inning short of being official, and the umpire insisted the Missions continue play, as Union Station was only a short distance from the ballpark. When Hammond refused, the umpire forfeited the game to the Buccaneers, resulting in an argument that did, in fact, cause San Antonio to miss its connection. The next day, Hammond officially protested to J. Alvin Gardner, insisting the game be resumed when the two teams met again on August 8. Shearn Moody answered Hammond's protest adamantly.

"Hammond started this ridiculous business of refusing to play, and we'll continue it!" Moody commented, claiming victory in accordance with the umpire's authority. When President Gardner sided with Hammond and directed Galveston to finish the game or forfeit, Moody grew livid. His anger boiled over just two days later, when transportation issues again interfered with the Bucs during a road trip to Dallas.

While most baseball executives considered railroad the transportation of choice, some believed bus travel might be more economical. Always the financial analyst, Shearn Moody ran the numbers and agreed, noting the Bucs would save $300 on their road trip to North Texas by chartering a bus. All went well until the bus broke down between Huntsville and Corsicana. The resulting late arrival in Dallas triggered an automatic forfeit to the Giants. For the second time in three days, Moody's team suffered the fate, not of the game's rulebook, but of the transportation system serving Texas.

Texas League owners who had sung the virtues of bus travel snickered secretly—better Moody's franchise be the guinea pig than one of their own. After all, Shearn could afford the financial hit, and his experiment taught other owners a valuable lesson: though bus travel may have been the wave of the future, it had yet to equal the railroad in terms of reliability. Instead of thanking Moody for taking a chance on what turned out to be a bad idea, fellow owners chastised him in the press as a penny-pincher.

Galveston's two transportation-related forfeits drew league-wide interest, but Shearn Moody's early season decision regarding ticket prices created controversy as well. Less than a month into the season and with attendance already lagging, Moody cut ticket prices by twenty-five cents each. Box seat tickets sold for one dollar, with other seats as low as a quarter. Moody hoped the price cut would increase attendance by 40 percent, his estimate of what it would take for his team to break even financially. But he erred from a public relations standpoint when restricting the Knothole Gang, along with women, to free admission on just Mondays and Fridays. The drop in Knothole Gang attendance especially impacted the enthusiasm at the ballpark, and it seemed to pull the team's spirits down as well.

Just a few days later, Del Pratt told the *Galveston Daily News*, "By gravy, I still insist I have the best ball club I ever managed…I can't see why we don't win."

To an extent, Pratt had a point. During the season's first half, his pitching staff led the league with twelve shutouts, yet the Bucs' offense failed to score a run in eight games, also leading the league. Team morale and prospects suffered further in early August when Shearn Moody released Preacher Thurman for refusing a pay cut. Thurman did not have the same financial wits as his owner and failed to see his individual success as having no impact on ticket sales.

At season's end, Pratt's early prophecy of the Bucs being an "If" team proved true. "If" they had gotten off to a better start, the season may have turned out differently, and "if" they'd had better fielding, perhaps the pitchers and batting would have led them to more victories. Unfortunately for Pratt, none of the "ifs" fell in his favor. "If" they had, perhaps Del Pratt would have kept his job.

Victor Emanuel's lavishing praise on Moody and the Bucs faded early in the season. He soon realized Galveston lacked talent, and the sportswriter's reputation took a hit. In late May, with the Bucs mired in a thirty-three-inning scoreless streak, Emanuel may have taken his criticism a step too far. Lamenting the team's poor play during three consecutive 2–0 losses, he sarcastically began his column noting how the crowd "swelled" beyond 250 paying customers. Likewise, by the end of his second paragraph, he called the 2–0 losses "loathsome" and reminded readers that the Bucs had scored only one run in the previous fifty innings.

When Emanuel spotlighted the Bucs' silent bats and implied a lack of effort to obtain better players in his "Walking the Plank" column, someone probably should have reminded the *GDN* sports editor that his boss just happened to own the team he covered for a living. After his May 26 rant,

Victor Emanuel's name disappeared from the Galveston sports pages. Whether he had become too critical for Shearn Moody's tastes is unknown, as no mention of his departure can be found. But as grandson Bobby Moody noted, "I wouldn't be a bit surprised if he crossed the line. Shearn Moody had a reputation as an 'it's my way or no way' manager. If he thought a reporter was hurting Galveston or a Moody interest, little doubt they would not have lasted long."

Despite an improved 67-86 record and sixth-place finish, the Buccaneers remained uncompetitive. For Victor Emanuel's prediction of a pennant within four years to come true, something had to change, and it had to change soon.

An early sign of coming success arrived in August when longtime Texas League official Joe Gardner gave Buck Fausett his endorsement as the league's top prospect.

"If I had a ball club, I'd grab that boy," Gardner said. "But he'd never see third base or any other position on the infield or outfield. He has the sweetest-looking arm of a catcher I've seen in years. If he could learn it, he would make out among the greatest catchers ever developed in this league."

Shearn Moody paid little attention to Gardner's comments and, in turn, earned his pitching staff's thanks. After a full game of catching Buck's throws from home plate, a pitcher would end up on the injured list with a swollen hand.

6
INVESTING IN THE FUTURE

For all Del Pratt's credentials as a player and motivator, he posted only one winning season in eight summers managing the Waco-Galveston franchise. As the unsuccessful 1932 campaign closed, Shearn Moody decided the time had come for a change. After all, change seemed the one constant in Shearn's life.

Just a year earlier, Shearn had married Frances Russell in San Diego. Some say the Moody family did not care for Shearn's choice of a bride, finding her too flamboyant and eager for attention. A Southern Methodist University graduate, Frances's stunning appearance earned her SMU "beauty" honors, and when she married the dashing Moody, the couple became among the most photogenic in Texas.

Whether historians have been fair to Frances or the Moody family in claiming she was shunned is questionable. Moody critics' claims that Frances had been previously married and brought children to the Moody home are patently false. Miss Russell, the granddaughter of a Kansas physician and daughter of a successful businessman, grew up attending the prestigious Ward-Belmont School in Nashville, Tennessee, and the Hockaday School for Girls. Adding four years at SMU to her education, simple arithmetic helps dispel many of the rumors. Still, some authors have written that Moody family members "loathed" Shearn's wife. But late in her life, the Moodys recognized Frances as the "right hand of the Moody family's key business patriarchs."

According to Doug McLeod, associated with the Moody family for well over fifty years:

Newlyweds Shearn and Frances Moody, 1931. *Courtesy of E. Douglas McLeod/Moody Archives.*

Frances was likely guilty of fibbing about her age; she was perhaps as many as three years older than some of the later records reflect. Frances was a beautiful young woman, inside and out; and, as an older stateswoman, she was as gracious a person as one could meet. When she entered a room full of people, she would not "run to the most important person in the room." Rather, she would stop and talk to everyone in her path, whether a Congressman or a waiter. That was Frances. She was actually beloved by many.

McLeod admits there may have been "some jealousy and competitiveness among a few of the women in the family, like Shearn's sisters Mary and Libbie. But that was because [Frances] was so pretty, elegant and gracious. And at least in the Moody family, college-educated women at the time were not the norm."

If critics allege that Shearn's family despised Frances or if she never earned acceptance in the Galveston community, facts show she did remain a force in the Moody family and Galveston for nearly eight decades. As chair of the Moody Foundation, Frances oversaw many philanthropic efforts, and her legacy can be seen in Galveston today.

Less than a year after his wedding, Moody made a less important, though no less controversial, decision when dismissing Del Pratt as manager. Despite his lack of success, few questioned Pratt's knowledge of baseball or eye for talent. But Moody expected a fast track to a championship, and Pratt simply wasn't delivering. With the season over, plenty of managers would be in search of jobs.

Moody's search for Pratt's replacement took him to Chicago and Harry Grabiner. Grabiner, secretary and vice-president of the White Sox, had parlayed a position as a peanut vendor in the ballpark to the front office. Knowing Moody sought both a manager and a relationship with a major-league franchise, Grabiner recommended Billy Webb, a fellow Chicagoan he'd known since the two were kids on the streets in the early 1900s, for the manager's slot.

———•———

William Joseph Webb was born during the summer of 1895, the son of an Irishman who worked as a bartender and stenographer. Although playing only five major-league games, Webb possessed a keen eye for baseball talent. He brought a commanding, no-nonsense approach to the game, traits he must have inherited from his father, an immigrant who eventually became an Illinois state legislator.

Breaking into professional baseball in 1916 as a utility infielder with Duluth of the Northern League, Webb batted an unimpressive .264 his rookie season. The next year, with Birmingham of the Southern Association, he developed power and posted a respectable .934 fielding average. In Birmingham, he played for manager Carlton Molesworth, a longtime minor leaguer who first broke into baseball in 1895 with the Washington Nationals.

Like Billy Webb, Molesworth appeared only briefly in the Major Leagues, yet he played twenty years in the minors. After bouncing around the New York State League, Molesworth landed in 1906 with the Montgomery Black Sox of the Southern Association, where he batted .300 or better for three straight seasons. In 1908, he moved to upstate Alabama and joined the Birmingham Barons as player-manager, a position he held for the next fourteen seasons.

Billy Webb played for two years under Carlton Molesworth, probably learning more about the game than most players learned in a career. Webb's seasons in Birmingham sandwiched a year of active duty in the U.S. Navy during World War I. Surviving the Battle of Verdun as a chief petty officer involved in operating the U.S. Naval Railway ranked far higher than baseball on Webb's list of accomplishments. As an enlistee, he gained minor fame as Woodrow Wilson's personal escort during armistice talks. By the beginning of the 1919 season, though, Webb was far from the trench warfare of Europe, once again plugging a hole in the Birmingham Barons' infield.

After his second season in Birmingham, Webb left for the International League, where he spent the next nine seasons. His best years as a professional came with Buffalo in 1923–25, when he batted .318 with 175 extra base hits, including fifty-five home runs while serving as player-manager. Derailed by injury in 1926, Webb returned to the International League with Toronto the following season, but he never regained the success he'd achieved in Buffalo. In 1930–31, he took his management experience to Binghamton of the New York–Pennsylvania League. Though none of his four seasons as a manager led to anything better than a middle-of-the-pack finish, Webb's unblemished eye for talent led sportswriters to claim he could tell a ballplayer "by the way he dressed and undressed in the locker room." A friend of comedian W.C. Fields, Webb frequently likened his dedication to baseball to Fields's passion for whiskey. "If I were to drink, I'd do it like W.C. Fields," he said.

Even though he wasn't actively engaged in baseball in 1932, Webb, Harry Grabiner and other White Sox staff remained in touch. With Chicago seeking a minor-league affiliate and Galveston in search of an agreement with a major-league club, Grabiner reached out to Shearn Moody, offering Billy Webb a glowing recommendation to be the Bucs' new manager.

Billy Webb's hiring barely made the sports pages compared to the revolutionary changes Texas League owners planned. For most of its history, the league had played a split-season schedule, the winner of the first-half pennant playing the top club of the second-half for the championship. The format intended to provide renewed hope for fans of the "tail-enders," as all teams' records reset to 0-0 in early July. With a few exceptions, though, the good teams remained good while the poor teams again fell to the bottom of the standings.

As the 1933 season approached, Texas League officials boasted of the quality baseball being played in the state. The *Dallas Morning News* wrote of Texas League talent rivaling that of the well-respected American Association, just a step below the majors. J. Alvin Gardner declared every team financially sound for the first time in many seasons, and the baseball world finally respected Texas as a source of talent. Several owners, though, believed the split-season format had outlived its usefulness. Quality baseball circuits determined champions in season-long marathons rather than in two sprints. The new "Shaughnessy Plan" playoff format seemed the perfect fit for a league ready to take a step forward.

Francis Joseph Shaughnessy was born in Amboy, Illinois, in 1883. As a schoolboy, he excelled in football and baseball, eventually playing both sports at Notre Dame while earning dual degrees in pharmacy and law. Shaughnessy moonlighted as a professional baseball player under an assumed name in the Class D Leagues of the Midwest. In 1905, he signed with the Washington Senators, appearing in just one game before being sent to the minor leagues. Over the next nineteen seasons, Shaughnessy bounced from league to league, playing and managing at the same time. Even after his playing career ended, he remained in baseball, spending another decade as a manager in the International League.

While he specialized in baseball, Shaughnessy also remained involved in football, coaching during the off-season. The Shaughnessy name even turned up in professional ice hockey, as he coached the Ottawa Senators to the Stanley Cup finals despite never seeing a hockey game before his hiring. Ultimately, Shaughnessy moved to Canada and served in the Canadian armed forces during World War I. When the Great Depression arrived, he entered the world of finance as a Montreal stockbroker. Fortunately, he had sports to fall back on, and in 1932 he became general manager of the International League's Montreal Royals.

THE GALVESTON BUCCANEERS

By the time Shaughnessy reentered baseball, the Great Depression's pinch had taken its toll on the minor leagues. Attendance plummeted, and leagues folded mid-season, particularly when one team took a commanding lead in the standings. Shaughnessy proposed a new playoff system based on what he had learned from ice hockey. Rather than a winner-take-all format, the Shaughnessy Plan called for a number of teams to earn playoff spots, with regular season standings a means of seeding teams for the post-season.

Francis Shaughnessy initially proposed his playoff format to the International and Texas Leagues. Officially, the Texas League became the first professional circuit to adopt it, agreeing to test the plan in 1933. The International League did the same just three days later. Over the next several years, the Shaughnessy Plan became standard in minor-league baseball, with some adjustments along the way.

Shaughnessy recommended that four of the Texas League's eight teams qualify for the playoffs. The league eliminated its divided-season format, with all teams in competition for one of the top four slots. At season's end, the top seed would face the fourth in a five-game playoff series, with seeds two and three doing the same. The winners would advance to a seven-game final for the championship.

Shearn Moody lobbied heavily in favor of the new format. He believed professional baseball's founders intended the game to be played daily over a period of months. The split-season format's forgiveness of early season failures did not honor the intent of a season's first game to be just as important as its last. Furthermore, Shaughnessy designed his plan to keep more fans interested throughout the season. At worst, four cities would remain heavily invested in their teams through the first round of playoffs. At best, all eight teams would be in competition for at least one of the playoff slots as the season neared its conclusion.

Besides redesigning the method of determining a champion, Texas League officials tackled several other off-season issues for 1933. Some teams claimed evening attendance didn't offset the cost of playing under the lights and pressed for a schedule featuring day games. Although the Buccaneers had drawn big crowds at night, Galveston offered a nightlife unique among the league's cities. Owners also considered scheduling more off days for the players. In the early Texas League, an off day meant nothing but a loss of gate receipts, but when the league expanded into Oklahoma, long overnight train rides degraded competition. In 1933, each team's schedule included seven double-headers followed by an off day, allowing players to rest before reaching their next destination. Like everything else during the

Great Depression, adjustment to the times took center stage in everyday life and baseball.

In spite of the hardships the Great Depression presented worldwide, Galveston felt a lesser impact. Economic forces had little effect on vice-oriented businesses, and the Maceo establishments required a large number of employees. Likewise, the ultra-conservative business practices handed down from Colonel Moody allowed the family enterprises to weather the Depression better than most. As banks failed nationwide, not a single Galveston bank closed; in fact, when customers rushed to other Texas banks to withdraw their money, Moody assets steadily grew. Galveston residents respected the family's financial judgment and believed a Moody bank was less of a risk than stuffing cash in a mattress or cigar box. Likewise, Moody-owned companies like ANICO retained employees through the leanest years the nation ever experienced. While the Moodys could not provide pay increases and sometimes offered deferred compensation or stock options in lieu of cash, their employees did not fear for lay-offs, providing a peace of mind few other Americans enjoyed.

The Moodys maintained a low profile during the Depression. Will recalled his father's lessons in frugality and humility. While so many in the nation suffered, he reemphasized the family values. Throughout the Depression, the Moodys avoided driving expensive cars or being seen as living a lavish lifestyle. For all the criticism some historians make of the Moody family, the insinuation that they cared little for the needs of the less fortunate is perhaps the most unfair of all. From retaining employees to feeding the needy, the Moodys did all they could to shelter Galvestonians from economic downturn. And in 1933, the plan included offering affordable entertainment as a diversion for local baseball fans. For Shearn Moody, a successful effort meant fielding a team to captivate the city through the long, hot summer ahead.

7

EARLY RETURNS

Billy Webb and Del Pratt brought completely different personas to Moody Stadium. Pratt's fiery and outspoken managing style gave way to Webb's quiet and unassuming personality. Billy certainly wanted to field a winning team and managed aggressively, but he respected the league office, his employer, players and fans. Galveston came to regard Webb as the ultimate gentleman. With Texas League veteran Jack Mealey at his coaching side, the *Dallas Morning News* writers noted that the Buccaneers would fail only if Shearn Moody didn't provide Webb with quality players. As the season neared, Moody busily signed some of the best talent available in the minor leagues.

Although the White Sox never formally declared Galveston a minor-league affiliate, Shearn Moody made the best of his Chicago connections. Billy Webb's relationship with the White Sox essentially served as an unwritten agreement where Chicago optioned players to Galveston for development. The first group Chicago sent southward included Charlie English, the same player Del Pratt had released the prior spring.

Texas League owners had intended to save money in 1933 by signing player-managers, but only San Antonio and Houston actually followed through. Del Pratt, probably too old to keep "player" in his title, initially moved on to Lubbock of the West Texas–New Mexico League, and only a small pool of experienced player-managers existed. A rising tide of young talent entered the Texas League, and other teams hired traditional field managers. With a salary cap of $4,250 and only sixteen players allowed on a roster, most owners could afford the added cost.

"Chief" Euel Moore, a member of the 1933 Bucs, was the Texas League's first Native American player. *Author's collection.*

As the season approached, Billy Webb continued making roster moves with Shearn Moody's blessing. Despite leading Texas League third basemen in fielding errors, retaining Buck Fausett topped his list. Moody sweetened the deal by assuring Buck a job aboard a steamship in the off-season. Moody also approved trading Ed Carrol to Baltimore for first baseman Dick Goldberg and signed Lawrence French, a second baseman from Texas Tech. Webb brought veteran "Chief" Euel Moore to camp to provide maturity on an otherwise young pitching staff. But when camp opened, one of the Bucs' key players trained with the Aggie baseball club at Texas A&M, and Webb eagerly awaited his arrival.

Roy Chambers Bell signed with Shearn Moody after a stellar college career at Texas A&M, where he improved his sub-.300 batting average to .475 between seasons and earned All-American honors as an outfielder. When he left the Aggies in the spring of 1931, Bell signed with Galveston, playing 260 games over the next two seasons while maintaining a steady .274 average. But the return to his alma mater for preseason training seemed to put Bell in a groove—one he would eventually carry all the way to the Major Leagues.

Roy Bell, a descendant of revolutionaries who fought at San Jacinto and one of Stephen F. Austin's original three hundred Texas settlers, was born in 1907 in Bellville, northwest of Houston. The son of a postal worker, Bell had a penchant for following a local deliveryman of Bohemian descent on his daily routes, earning him the nickname "Beau." Beau's parents instilled the importance of education in their children, and after the eldest graduated from Texas A&M, the university became a Bell family tradition. To this day, when one Bell family member graduates, he or she takes personal responsibility to ensure that the next in line completes studies at the school.

When enrolling at Texas A&M, Beau Bell had little intention of playing professional baseball. Initially, he planned to follow his older brother in studying electrical engineering, but he changed his major to zoology in hopes of earning his doctorate and becoming a professor and coach. Later, he again changed his field of study to entomology.

When Buck Fausett joined the roster in 1932, he and Bell probably had numerous conversations about Buck's favorite insect, the boll weevil, and how it drove him off the

Before debuting for the Galveston Buccaneers, Beau Bell played for Texas A&M, the same university where he would coach baseball after retiring as a player. *Courtesy of Dianne Sides.*

farm. But in recalling his college days, Beau noted hunting as his only remaining interest in zoology, and mosquitoes eradicated any aspirations to become an entomologist. Little did he know he would spend the early years of his baseball career playing in Galveston, a historically mosquito-infested island.

Billy Webb's initial goal as the Bucs' manager meant stabilizing the roster. In Del Pratt's two years as manager, sixty-eight players appeared on the roster. Webb planned patience. Constantly juggling the lineup prevented the Bucs from developing as a team. He intended to set his roster in the spring and stick with it through the season. Webb first addressed a need at catcher, a position split among four players in 1932.

Maurice Francis "Jack" Mealey brought eight years of minor-league catching experience to Galveston. Mealey bounced from league to league over his career, playing twelve minor-league seasons across the country. A Pennsylvania native, the five-foot-nine, 165-pound catcher's frame made him smaller than most at his position, but he developed into one of the minor leagues' best overall catchers. At thirty-four years old, Mealey was among the oldest players on the roster, and Webb chose him to serve as second in command. But Mealey had never been particularly durable, averaging about eighty games a season over the course of his career, so Webb knew he needed versatility elsewhere on his roster.

Jack Mealey, Billy Webb and Beau Bell. *Courtesy E. Douglas McLeod/Moody Archives.*

In the infield, Webb signed first baseman Dick Goldberg, a twenty-eight-year-old with only a year of experience in professional baseball. Goldberg showed promise as a hitter and posted outstanding statistics defensively, addressing a major Galveston shortcoming. Webb started Charlie English at second base, a rare power hitter at the position with the ability to consistently hit for extra bases.

Shortstop Keith Molesworth fit perfectly into Webb's model of an athletic, educated baseball player. In 1932, Molesworth played 149 games with Waco and hit twenty home runs, power seldom seen in a shortstop. But Molesworth had interests far beyond baseball. At Monmouth College, he lettered in baseball, football, basketball and track, and in 1931, the same year he played as an original member of the Buccaneers, he earned a spot on George Halas's Chicago Bears. In two seasons in Galveston, Molesworth rarely missed an inning, posting a respectable batting average though unable to hit a single home run in Moody Stadium. Fresh off an NFL championship, Molesworth's bat did not concern Billy Webb, but he had proven to be a miserable fielder, committing 112 errors over his two seasons. Webb would be challenged to develop Molesworth defensively, an effort made all the more difficult by the suspect fielding of his double play partner, Charlie English.

Third baseman Buck Fausett rounded out the infield, returning for a second season in Galveston. Like his fellow infielders, Fausett batted above the league average, but his defensive skills remained raw, as he posted a fielding percentage of .901 in his first season. Billy Webb saw something in Fausett, though, and knew if his fielding improved at the same rate as his batting, his potential as a ballplayer would be unlimited.

In the outfield, Webb oversaw a tremendous upgrade. Releasing the entire 1932 outfield except for Beau Bell and Tony Governor, Webb promoted Governor to the starting lineup. He also signed Fuzzy Hufft, a longtime minor leaguer who had hit nearly two hundred home runs and batted .338 over the course of a career that carried him throughout the Midwest to the Pacific Coast League. But with Hufft's age and durability in question, Webb brought in Wally Moses, a twenty-two-year-old Georgia prospect who had shown potential in the field and at the plate with Monroe, Shreveport and Tyler in 1932.

With the Bucs coming off two seasons near the bottom of the Texas League standings, many expected Webb to overhaul the pitching staff. Statistically, though, the 1932 staff had not fared poorly. Led by Henry Thormahlen's twenty wins and Ed Carroll and George Darrow's fifteen each, the trio limited opponents to just over one base runner per inning. Considering the porous defense committed one and a half errors per game, many of those reaching base did so at no fault of the hurlers. All three pitchers returned for 1933, along with Euel Moore and the previously ineffective Frank Tubbs. Future major leaguers Orville Jorgens, Ira Hutchinson and Bill Chamberlain filled out the staff.

Webb penciled himself in to play if the Bucs got in a pinch and entered 1933 with a young, offensively explosive roster, respectable pitching and miserable defense. To bolster all three, he drilled the Bucs incessantly in the art of bunting from offensive, pitching and defensive perspectives. Few balls sailed over the fences in Moody Stadium, but its expansive outfield forced defenses to cover a lot of ground. Billy Webb expected the Bucs to get a lot of base hits in the ballpark, and his team's speed would be a weapon Webb would employ to move base runners into scoring position. As the season approached, Webb realized he fielded a team with challenges, and a serious run for the pennant probably wasn't in the cards. Neither he nor Shearn Moody realized how quickly the young team would gel.

Along with a new manager and revamped lineup, Shearn Moody brought a new sports editor to the *GDN* for 1933: William Van Fleet. A University of Texas journalism student still a semester from graduation, Van Fleet was lured by Moody to his newspaper before semester's end.

Bill Van Fleet, born in San Marcos in 1908, grew up in nearby Hondo, Texas. One of five children, Bill initially attended Schreiner College in Kerrville before moving to Austin, where he covered sports for the university's newspaper, the *Daily Texan*. UT athletes thought so highly of Van Fleet that they invited him to join the campus "Half Moon" athletic fraternity, despite

Bill Van Fleet. *Courtesy of Mary Van Fleet Williams.*

the fact that he wasn't particularly athletic himself. Apparently, Van Fleet's reputation reached all the way to Galveston, where Shearn Moody recruited him to replace Victor Emanuel. The young reporter immediately became a hit with readers, his "Here's the Dope" column providing news and insight into Galveston sports both on and off the field.

Unlike the previous two seasons, Galveston burst from the gate in 1933. By early May, Wally Moses led the league in batting, and Euel Moore boasted a 5-0 win-loss record. Attendance increased rapidly as the Bucs transformed from the Texas League's worst hitting team to its best in short order. Buck Fausett received high marks from Billy Webb and the Texas League press, who listed him among the league's most improved players.

In the meantime, on May 23, Shearn Moody added to his growing list of responsibilities when Frances gave birth to their first child, Shearn Jr. The newest member of the Moody family may not have been responsible for the Bucs' change of fortunes, but something fueled a seemingly tireless lineup. While the rest of the league waited for Galveston to cool off, at the end of May, Buccaneers' bats showed no sign of fatigue. Wally Moses led the Texas League in batting average, as did Buck Fausett's fifty-nine base hits. Beau Bell, Dick Goldberg, Charlie English and Fausett had each posted double-digit hitting streaks, and pitchers Euel Moore and George Darrow led the league with seven wins each. The Bucs' speed accounted for twenty-six triples in less than eight weeks. Still, as spring turned to summer, Galveston barely clung to fourth place, ever important under the Shaughnessy playoff plan.

Despite impressive individual statistics, early in the season Galveston proved to be an inconsistent, streaky team. Three extended losing streaks all came to an end behind George Darrow's pitching. By the end of June, Darrow's 15-3 record primarily had led Galveston's rise to second place in the standings, well ahead of fifth-place Dallas. With the season's final two months about to get underway, the suddenly overachieving Buccaneers surprised even their most ardent supporters, Billy Webb and Shearn Moody.

Not only did Bucs' pitchers post big numbers, but also the best pitching in the Texas League rested with the four southern clubs. Galveston, Houston, Beaumont and San Antonio hurlers claimed the twelve lowest ERAs in the league, with George Darrow, Euel Moore and Orville Jorgens among the leaders. *Dallas Morning News* sportswriter George White declared Darrow the top prospect in the Texas League. Still, Houston opened a nine-game lead over the Buccaneers in the standings. Although the Bucs held a firm grip on second place and a playoff spot, all was not well at Moody Stadium.

Galveston fans had a knack for consistent grumbling over umpiring. Beat writer Bill Van Fleet didn't accuse umpires of being partial to certain teams or players; rather, he believed Texas League umpires to be less skilled than those of other leagues. A mid-month swoon brought the issue to a head at Moody Stadium.

In the midst of a four-game home losing streak, everyone in Moody Stadium—including the fans, managers, players and even the Knothole Gang—took their frustrations out on the umpires. While dropping a twin bill to Dallas, the plate umpire's inconsistent strike zone enraged both Billy Webb and catcher Jack Mealey. The two held a heated discussion with the umpire, and as they argued, fans tossed a barrage of soda bottles and eggs onto the field. Despite Stan Elbert's recollection of his Knothole Gang's impeccable behavior, news accounts noted even the kids got in on the action.

With Webb and Mealey tossed from the game, the umpires knew reaching the safety of their dressing room posed a stiff challenge. Umpires passed through an opening in the bleachers when leaving Moody Stadium's field, and the bleachers attracted the most rowdy fans. An umpire reaching the dressing room without being drenched or soiled with whatever garbage the crowd had on hand became as rare as a member of the Knothole Gang skipping church. On occasion, arguing even spilled into the stands, and fans engaged in fistfights among themselves. A fan base enjoying the city's best baseball season in nearly thirty years seemed to have lost focus on the pennant race. One wrote to Bill Van Fleet that fans saw their team headed from the top of the heap to the cellar, and they didn't want to get left behind.

The Bucs didn't limit their feuding to home games. On July 28, in pre-game warm-ups in Dallas, the Bucs and Steers engaged in one of the Texas League's most notorious outbursts. During batting practice, Galveston's sparsely used catcher Ed Connolly grew tired of Dallas's Sal Gliatto's heckling. A veteran pitcher, Gliatto ranked among the best in the minors over the previous six seasons. At one point, Gliatto apparently touched a nerve and "Connolly…came back with an uncomplimentary remark about Gliatto's ancestors, and the pitcher went him one better, whereupon they came together." Gliatto and his 150-pound frame offered no match for the Brooklyn-raised Connolly. Sal left the ballpark a few minutes later, bruised and with loosened teeth. To further increase the tension, Fuzzy Hufft picked up a groundskeeper's rake to defend his teammate but inexplicably struck the elderly groundskeeper over the head. When the dust settled, Dallas had lost its best pitcher for the season with a broken thumb and jaw. Hufft and Frank Tubbs returned to the ballpark a day later in a "condition unbecoming to the national pastime," disgusting both the Steers and their fans.

With Dallas scheduled to visit Moody Stadium two weeks later, concern for player, umpire and fan safety built in the Texas League office. Moody Stadium lacked the level of security in Dallas, and fans could "take liberties" with players and umpires alike. To calm the swelling resentment between the teams and Galveston fans, Shearn Moody scheduled a player appreciation night during the series, with an evening's gate receipts to be split among those on the Bucs' roster. Surely, the incentive of playing before an appreciative crowd and an extra paycheck would outweigh any anger the Bucs still held toward their opponents. J. Alvin Gardner further helped diffuse the situation by deploying four umpires to work the series as opposed to the usual two. More eyes meant fewer missed calls, and a well-umpired game would calm both the teams and the crowd. Likewise, Gardner publicly complimented Galveston and its fans as "spunky competitors." The Bucs opened the season with what many rated the worst roster in the Texas League, but Billy Webb had built his team into a contender and almost a sure bet to make the playoffs.

Before the Dallas series, the Bucs gained ground on first-place Houston. When the Steers did arrive in town, 4,200 fans turned out to watch Galveston come back from a 3–0 deficit and beat Dallas on Jack Mealey's ninth-inning home run in the first game. With the win, the Bucs pulled even with Houston. After Dallas took the second game, the Bucs bounced back to peacefully win the final by a 3–1 score. What turned out to be an anticlimactic series didn't still the concern of the rest of the league over Galveston's fan base.

Bill Van Fleet recalled a discussion among the umpires, President Gardner and the Dallas manager during the series in which all agreed that Galveston fans were the toughest in the league. Describing them as "rabid," all admired their enthusiasm. Still, the umpires agreed that fan reaction had no impact on the way they called a game. Frank Coe, notoriously eager to eject players who objected to his calls, noted any player making objectionable comments would be put out of the game regardless of the player, the team or the venue. He added that every ballplayer whose manager asked what he said to get tossed from a game answered, "I didn't say anything, Coach."

Despite fan behavior and fears of physical violence during the Dallas series, Billy Webb tried to keep his team focused on the pennant race. Tied for the league lead and seventeen games ahead of fourth-place Beaumont, the Bucs had already qualified for the Shaughnessy playoffs, but positioning in the standings remained up for grabs. Although a sizable gap existed between Houston and Galveston and third- and fourth-place Dallas and San Antonio, Billy Webb wanted to avoid any distraction a playoff series with Dallas might create. With San Antonio sitting in fourth place, a series against the Bronchos would likely mean Galveston's moving from worst to first in the Texas League over a two-year span. Billy Webb brought stability to the franchise, and Shearn Moody could not have been more pleased with the results.

While Webb attempted to maintain focus, Buck Fausett decided to take a major step during the season's most important stretch of games. On the road in Oklahoma City, Fausett married twenty-two-year-old Ann Sindik, a New York native, almost exactly two years after Shearn Moody had married Frances. Of course, in 1931 the bottom-feeding Buccaneers didn't have to worry about the playoffs, and it is likely Webb wasn't completely pleased with Buck's timing. While it may not have distracted the team, it certainly distracted Fausett.

Immediately following the Dallas series, the Bucs lost Euel Moore, his 2.67 ERA and seventeen wins for the season to a ruptured appendix. Moore formed half of the best one-two pitching combination in the Texas League, with George Darrow as his counterpart. Though losing fifteen of his thirty-five starts, in six of those losses the Bucs came up short by a single run. As Galveston made its final push for playoff seeding and the $1,000 cash prize for taking the championship, Bill Webb focused on the task ahead: qualifying for the Dixie Series with whatever players he had available.

The Dixie Series began in 1920 to add a layer of competition among the minor leagues. Pitting the Texas League and Southern Association champions against each other in a seven-game contest, the Dixie Series had become a fight for minor-league supremacy in the South. Through 1932, the Texas League dominated the series, taking all but three trophies. The Fort Worth Panthers ruled the Dixie Series, in each of the first six series winning five and then adding another win in 1930. The New Orleans Pelicans appeared in three Dixie Series for the Southern Association but lost each time. As the 1933 series approached, the Southern Association defended two consecutive trophies, Birmingham having defeated Houston in 1931 and Chattanooga dominating Beaumont in

1932. Texas League president J. Alvin Gardner desperately wanted to prove his league as among the best in all of baseball, and the Dixie Series played an important role in his efforts.

Jabez Alvin Gardner was born in the Southeast Texas town of Colmesneil in 1890. Though ultimately making his fortune in the oil business, at age six Gardner moved to Beaumont with his family and attended public schools. In his early teens, he served as batboy for the Beaumont Exporters. Just a few years later, he began a seventeen-year career with Gulf Oil, spending time in Mexico and helping to organize a city baseball league. Over the years, Gardner lived in several Texas League cities and, by 1920, had purchased

J. Alvin Gardner served as Texas League president from 1929 to 1954. *Author's collection.*

stock in the Wichita Falls Spudders franchise. In 1925, Gardner resigned from Gulf Oil to join his brother in a private drilling business and became director of the Wichita Falls club. Within a year, he purchased a majority interest in the Spudders, ultimately selling in 1929 just before the Great Depression arrived. Still, Gardner was not finished with the Texas League.

In October 1929, longtime league president Doak Roberts became increasingly ill. Roberts, with Texas League ties dating to the nineteenth century, had become well respected throughout baseball as an executive and talent scout. Over the years, he held ownership in many franchises and discovered a number of players, including future Hall of Famer Tris Speaker, whom Roberts signed to the 1906 champion Cleburne Railroaders midway through the city's only year in the league. Roberts served stints as league president throughout his career, eventually assuming the position full time in 1920. When his health failed, owners searched for a capable temporary replacement, electing J. Alvin Gardner to serve in his absence. Roberts's illness turned out to be short but fatal, as he passed away in late November. League owners reconvened and voted to keep Gardner on for a five-year term. The success of the Texas League during his reign as president turned five years into a quarter century at the helm of one of baseball's most storied minor-league circuits.

Owners knew Gardner as a fair man, dealing suspensions and rulings only after fully investigating matters at hand. Despite his admiration for Shearn Moody, Gardner engaged in more than one controversy with Buccaneers management, including the August 1933 incident with Dallas. Disciplinary actions involving Galveston players regularly crossed his desk, and Gardner responded with impartial rulings, often infuriating the local fan base. But Shearn Moody knew Gardner's support had been instrumental in bringing the Texas League back to Galveston. Likewise, while the league had suffered under the control of financially unstable organizations, Gardner knew someone of Moody's wealth and business sense would be the cornerstone of a stable league. With or without fan support, he recognized Moody had the resources and personal drive to build a successful franchise. With the Bucs' rapid rise to the top of the standings, his assumptions about Shearn Moody had proven correct.

After tying Houston for the Texas League lead in mid-August, the Bucs slipped four games behind a week later, crippled by the loss of Euel Moore and an ankle injury to pitcher Henry Thormahlen. Though still resting comfortably in second place, for the season's final two weeks, Houston and Galveston played to a standstill, the Bucs six and a half games out of first place going into a last-day doubleheader against the Buffaloes. Unfortunately, a storm heading up the Gulf Coast from South Texas washed out any chance the Bucs had to bolster their confidence heading into the playoffs and a first-round matchup with Dallas. The pennant-winning Houston Buffaloes placed their 94-57 record on the line against fourth place San Antonio. As the Shaughnessy Plan intended, fans in all four cities clung to hopes of a championship.

With the playoffs just two days away, Billy Webb faced a significant problem at shortstop. Keith Molesworth, scheduled to leave for Chicago to join George Halas's Bears the day after the season ended, had not expected the Bucs to qualify for the post-season. Though Molesworth's fielding had cost Galveston some games, he provided a steady bat all season, and Webb didn't have a suitable substitute on his roster. League rules prevented replacing players late in the season, so Webb's only alternative to Molesworth would be to play in his place. Fortunately, the day before Game 1 against Dallas, George Halas granted Molesworth a delay in reporting to Chicago.

Before the playoffs, Texas League sportswriters handed out awards and selected the season's top players. Galveston's Buck Fausett, Tony Governor and George Darrow earned spots on the all-star team, and Darrow took the Most Valuable Pitcher prize. For his season-long efforts, Darrow received a fifty-dollar cash prize.

As Dallas and Galveston prepared for their series, Bill Van Fleet examined statistics and recognized how evenly the two teams were matched. Though Galveston was the favorite to take the series, its regular season record against Dallas was only 12-10, with Dallas outscoring the Bucs 93–92. Dallas held a .252–.242 batting average over Galveston, though the Bucs bested the Steers in hits, 180–177. Six of the games had been settled by a single run, with Dallas pitching earning the only shutout. Had it not been for Euel Moore's illness, the Bucs would have gone into the series with a substantial advantage among pitchers. Moore and Darrow had led the team to three wins each over the Steers, followed by Henry Thormahlen's 2-2 record. The rest of the staff posted a win each, but Tubbs and Orville Jorgens had each lost to Dallas three times. With Jorgens scheduled to pitch for Galveston in the first game in Dallas, he and Billy Webb both considered a good performance vital to set the tone for the series.

The first-round series held true to Van Fleet's analysis. Stretching for the full five games, Galveston came from a 2-1 deficit to advance to the championship series, with Ira Hutchinson's and Orville Jorgen's pitching leading the way.

Perhaps the ruse of the Dallas series turned out to be a widely publicized rift between Billy Webb and Shearn Moody. Down two games to one, news reports claimed that Webb reminded Moody of the bonus he had been promised should he lead Galveston to the playoffs. For his part, Moody seemed to have a case of selective memory. An incensed Webb went to his office and returned with a written contract Moody had signed early in the season. Shearn relented.

Shearn Moody made headlines complaining about Dallas first baseman Zeke Bonura being voted Texas League MVP. Bonura's .357 batting average, 24 home runs, 141 runs scored and 111 RBIs certainly offered the credentials, but Moody countered that the entire Buccaneers' infield had played every game of the season, and Buck Fausett led the league with 192 hits. Whether Moody and Webb purposely intended their dispute and rant over the MVP award to distract Dallas before facing the Bucs in a must-win Game 4 is unknown, but clearly the owner and manager had led the Steers to view Galveston as a team in disarray. If a ruse had been planned, it worked to perfection.

While Dallas and Galveston took their series to the wire, the fourth-place Missions finished off regular pennant-winning Houston in short order. Though the Missions had beaten Houston in just six of twenty-two games in the season, they came alive in the playoffs. Completely dominating the Buffaloes, San Antonio swept the first three games and qualified for a spot against Galveston for the championship. The Missions peaked at just the right moment, and Billy Webb knew a Buccaneer trip to the Dixie Series was no foregone conclusion. His suspicions proved correct, as San Antonio maintained its momentum in taking the series four games to two. San Antonio's Texas League championship had proven the effectiveness of the Shaughnessy playoff system. In its first season, the format provided a major upset, as the fourth-place team pulled out an unlikely victory. Fans in Galveston and Dallas were disappointed, and those in Houston were enraged. But the system proved any team had a chance if it could stay in the running for fourth place until season's end.

For Galveston, the loss to San Antonio represented a bitter end to an extremely sweet season. Upon arriving home, the 1933 Bucs players immediately began to leave the island for the off-season. Keith Molesworth headed for Chicago, where he would captain the Bears to a second NFL championship. Several other players boarded trains to join their respective major-league ball clubs for the remainder of the year. Those remaining became the toast of the town with Shearn Moody, Billy Webb and other Buccaneers invited to banquets at a variety of venues. Buck Fausett set off to work on Shearn Moody's steamboat for the off-season, while Beau Bell, George Darrow, Tony Governor and Fuzzy Hufft all made plans to remain on the island. Their presence during the off-season showed a loyalty pleasing to the Buccaneers' front office.

While Shearn Moody undoubtedly controlled the Buccaneers' purse strings, he gave great latitude to team vice-president Roy Koehler and secretary Sam Jack Evans. In fact, the two executives, along with Billy Webb, could be largely credited with building the Galveston roster.

Sam Jack Evans arrived in Galveston in 1931 along with the Waco franchise. Evans spent two decades managing Waco's Cotton Palace, a sporting and events center hosting events ranging from carnivals to football games. The facility accommodated horse racing, boxing and baseball, as well, not to mention entertainers and circus acts. Evans claimed "millions" of people attended events at the Cotton Palace, the largest single event drawing seventy-five thousand spectators.

Friends and co-workers knew Sam Jack as a wisecracking master of sarcasm and humor. The Moody House newsletter lauded his ability to work associates into a fit of rage before ultimately injecting a "hearty laugh that moves all the way down then up the ribs, turns over the tickle box and leaves the heart strings strumming a happier note."

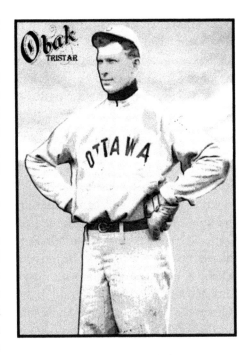

Frank Shaughnessy. *Author's collection.*

Evans held no interest in baseball until 1912, when rookie Detroit Tiger Del Pratt visited his Waco home. The two remained friends over the years, and when Waco interests purchased the Galveston Sand Crabs in 1924, Pratt and Evans agreed to manage team affairs on and off the field. Evans, more of a businessman than a baseball executive, turned the Cubs into a profitable organization not on the field but as a broker of player contracts. Evans signed several of Del Pratt's recruits at low salaries and eventually parlayed them into lucrative profits when selling their rights to higher-level teams. While the strategy profited Cubs owners to a small extent, the unsustainable practice interfered with any chance of on-field success. Constant roster turnover prevented players from coming together as a team, and lack of success dampened gate receipts. Evans continued to please team owners by selling any sort of talent for immediate cash, and the fan base grew tired of the practice. Any profits from player development coincided with dropping ticket sales, and eventually Evans's financial reports swam with red ink.

When the Cubs moved to Galveston, Shearn Moody liked Evans's style. Whether he thought of a ball club as a "brokerage firm" of sorts is unknown, but Moody quickly picked up on Evans's methods. Moody amazed sportswriters with the prices others paid for Buccaneer contracts. When Moody replaced Del Pratt after two unsuccessful seasons, Evans remained in Galveston and continued his profitable ways.

Galveston fans loved Sam Jack Evans, and the feeling was mutual. He believed Galveston to have the most loyal and baseball-intelligent fans in the league. Players also admired him, both as a businessman and as a rung on their career ladder. Evans's list of Galveston signees and eventual contract sales included Orville Jorgens, a pitcher he described as so cold-blooded "he wouldn't bleed if he cut his own finger." He nicknamed Ed Connolly "One Round" after his skirmish with Sal Gliatto in Dallas, stating the catcher was "ready to start slinging fists any time, any place, and will even name the place and time." Evans also had high regard for Charlie English, "a ladies' fancy"; Keith Molesworth; and Beau Bell. But he saved his greatest praise for Buck Fausett, noting he would be the most valuable Buccaneer in coming seasons. Whether he meant value on the baseball diamond or in Shearn Moody's bank account remains a question, but Evans's history suggests the latter.

Ever the promoter, after Galveston's unexpected 1933 success, Evans rambled off a lengthy list of little-known Buccaneer facts:

- Galveston drew more fans to road games than any team in the Texas League.
- Even though opposing managers and players dreaded the Bucs' arrival, owners anxiously awaited the ticket sales accompanying them.
- Galveston received more publicity in out-of-town newspapers than any other team.
- The Bucs had literally been "hamstrung" throughout the season. The team was plagued with charley horses, bad ankles and sore arms all season. Dick Goldberg played all year with a chronic and painful hamstring injury, Buck Fausett played despite a recurring bout of the flu, Charlie English finished the schedule with a fractured toe and Wally Moses's ankle never fully healed from an early season injury.
- The Shaughnessy playoff format profited Galveston more than any other team.
- Keith Molesworth played every inning of every game.
- A core of Bucs fans attended every 1933 home game, and a number traveled with the team on road trips.

Sam Jack Evans may have arrived as an outsider to the Moody family enterprises, but Roy Koehler had been a close associate for over two decades.

A Galveston native, Koehler began working for the Moodys in 1910 as a cotton press watchman. When Will Moody recognized his dedication in chasing people he did not believe belonged from the grounds, he promoted Koehler to cotton press manager. The community held equal respect, and Koehler volunteered for a number of efforts, including the Galveston Bible Class, the annual "empty stocking" drive for needy children at Christmas, the Galveston Kiwanis Club, community Easter egg hunts and the Elks bowling team, and served as vice-president of the Galveston Baseball Association.

During his time as compress manager, Koehler realized the difficulty of bagging baled cotton. With an entrepreneurial spirit the Moodys must have loved, Koehler founded the Dependable Bag and Bagging Company. His firm grew to employ sixteen, selling a variety of cotton press supplies. In 1928, a seemingly prophetic Koehler sold a large portion of the business just prior to the start of the Great Depression and his remaining interests four years later.

When Shearn Moody first considered bringing professional baseball back to Galveston, he turned to Roy Koehler for guidance. Koehler managed the planning and construction of Moody Stadium and impressed Moody with his baseball knowledge. In fact, Moody became so impressed that he appointed Koehler to handle baseball matters for the franchise. Koehler first lobbied for nighttime baseball in Galveston, realizing fans would prefer to watch a game during the cool evenings rather than in the stifling midday heat. Galvestonians realized they had the best ballpark in the Texas League, and most recognized Roy Koehler as the mastermind—backed, of course, by Shearn Moody's bankroll.

Galveston Buccaneers vice-president Roy Koehler.
Courtesy E. Douglas McLeod/Moody Archives.

In 1932, Koehler attended the National Association of Baseball Clubs annual meeting in Columbus with the intention of luring the convention to Galveston the following year. While in Ohio, Koehler met Billy Webb, the same Billy Webb whom Harry Grabiner would recommend Shearn Moody hire as manager less than a year later.

Not only did Koehler succeed in attracting the baseball convention to Galveston, filling the Moody hotels, but he also developed relationships paving the way for successful baseball to return to the city. The Moodys were intensely loyal to Roy Koehler, and the loyalty was mutual. Shearn Moody, Roy Koehler and Sam Jack Evans became among the shrewdest executives in all of minor-league baseball. With Billy Webb handling field duties in 1934, they all looked forward to an even greater season.

8

ONE SPLENDID SEASON

Off-Season, 1934

By January 1934, the Buccaneers' front office was dealing with the struggles facing every minor-league team without a major-league affiliation. Euel Moore, Keith Molesworth, Charlie English and Dick Goldberg signed elsewhere, with faint hopes that English might return if he didn't make the Chicago White Sox roster. The Texas League's other independent clubs, Tulsa and Oklahoma City, sold a number of players for cash as well. The rest of the league awaited the end of spring training to find out which players their big-league affiliates would assign them. As they waited, Shearn Moody went on a spending spree to fill out a roster with several components of the 1933 pennant chase still intact.

By the end of January, Roy Koehler had announced contract offers to nineteen players, including the entire 1933 starting lineup with the exception of Molesworth, English and Goldberg. The pitching staff required an overhaul as several members of the 1933 team took their careers elsewhere.

Monty Stratton, a six-foot-five pitcher from Hunt County in North Texas, signed early in the year. Billy Webb described Stratton as the "dark horse" of the staff with minimal experience but a fastball and curve that Red River Valley league batters had found unhittable the previous season. Hailing from Greenville, Stratton's height intimidated opposing batters as he released the ball from a point far above home plate level. Adding even more height to his staff, Webb signed six-foot-six Joe Gibbs. A former high school football star, Gibbs also brought limited experience to the staff, having pitched professionally in just five games in 1931. The lanky son of a Baptist minister, Gibbs showed tremendous promise in the amateur ranks, and Webb believed hitters facing both Gibbs and Stratton in the same series would be dumbfounded by the unusual angles at which their pitches arrived from the mound.

Based less on talent than pedigree, the Bucs signed Merritt Hubbell, the brother of future Hall of Fame pitcher Carl Hubbell. With five years of minor-league experience, Merritt started twenty-nine games for Baton Rouge in 1932, posting a 13-11 record and a suspect ERA. Billy Webb turned to another baseball family when signing Glenn Liebhardt, son of the

Harry Gumbert led the Galveston pitching staff during the 1934 season. *Author's collection.*

former Cleveland pitcher of the same name who posted an ERA of just 2.17 over four seasons early in the century. Liebhardt had played with Billy Webb's Toronto club three years earlier and impressed the manager enough to earn an invitation to Galveston.

Orville Jorgens had settled into the Bucs' rotation after spending the previous four seasons with ten teams. A Chicago native like Merritt Hubbell, Jorgens had a more accomplished brother, Arnot, who spent ten years as a New York Yankees utility player.

Harry "Gunboat" Gumbert became the Bucs' most important off-season signing. In four previous minor-league seasons, the Pennsylvania native won forty-six games and had proven a workhorse able to pitch well over two hundred innings in a season if needed. Gumbert had a reputation for allowing base runners, but with Galveston's potent offense, Billy Webb expected his pitchers to merely keep the Bucs close until they outscored their opponents.

While the Bucs signed a number of quality pitchers, holes remained in the infield and at catcher. With Dick Goldberg and Keith Molesworth in Baltimore and Jack Mealey preparing for his twelfth season behind the plate, Webb looked for youthful experience. He found his first baseman in Joe Malay, a Brooklyn native who spent a portion of the 1933 season with the New York Giants. Malay played professionally for eight teams and routinely batted above .300. Though lacking power, he brought defensive skill to a Buccaneers infield that ranked among the league's worst for three consecutive seasons.

At catcher, Billy Webb called on veteran Bob Linton, a thirty-two-year-old Arkansan who played one major-league season with the Pittsburgh Pirates. In his other six professional seasons, Linton searched for a home with eight teams, always posting a solid batting average for a catcher, along with stellar defensive statistics. Linton and Mealey both offered similar skill sets and had reached the point in their careers when catchers could thrive as platoon players.

As the season approached, only shortstop remained a glaring need. Although Keith Molesworth's glove surrendered nearly as many runs as he scored, he had a powerful bat for a shortstop, never missed an inning and shined in the 1933 playoffs. Webb brought in three players to compete for the job, and by spring training's end, young Don Robertshaw, a Duke University graduate, had beat out Len Shires. Robertshaw, who signed with the Philadelphia Athletics after college, found the jump to the majors a challenge his first spring, so he spent the last two seasons honing his skills in the minors. For his part, Len Shires offered a serviceable back-up option and also held a superior knowledge of baseball, leading Webb to assign him third-base coaching duties.

Though the Bucs returned the best outfield in the Texas League with Moses, Bell and Tony Governor, Shearn Moody went for broke in signing former major leaguer Moose Clabaugh. A veteran of eleven professional seasons, Clabaugh hit below .300 only twice, with his 180 home runs a bonus. He hit for extra bases as often as singles and provided surprising speed on the base paths. Like many of his new teammates, Clabaugh struggled defensively, but he provided the near complete package for which a manager yearned on his roster. With Clabaugh on board, Galveston arguably sported the best batting lineup in the Texas League.

Once again, Billy Webb placed his faith in smart ballplayers for the 1934 season, signing as many high school graduates and players with college experience as he could find. The outstanding outfield and powerful bat of Buck Fausett received a major boost when the White Sox optioned Charlie English back to Galveston. Pitching and defense would once again determine the Bucs' success.

Spring Training and Roster Adjustments

Webb arranged a five-game home exhibition series with the American Association's Toledo Mud Hens as a warm-up for the Texas League schedule. Though Toledo had played poorly in recent seasons, Webb believed an unfamiliar opponent would be a test for how the Bucs might fair in the season's early going. Unfortunately, the series did not build confidence for either the team or Billy Webb.

Toledo took four of the five games in Galveston, and in three, the Bucs provided little competition. Galveston exhibited its continuing defensive issues, committing thirteen errors in the series. Orville Jorgens racked up four of his own while pitching just four innings in a game turning out to be the Bucs' only win of the series.

Days before the season opener in San Antonio, the Bucs lifted their spirits, taking out their frustrations on the American Association's Columbus Red Birds in a 13–1 win, despite adding six errors to their pre-season total. In final preparation for the season opener at San Antonio, Webb scheduled a game with a local amateur team, the I-E Queen team. Though committing another two errors, the Bucs dominated and beat the amateurs 10–0. The plethora of fielding errors served as the most glaring statistic of the pre-season schedule, the Bucs having committed twenty-one miscues in just seven games. If the team had any chance to compete in 1934, the defense had to step up its game.

Although Webb knew his team needed to improve in many areas, both he and Sam Jack Evans spoke highly of the roster. Evans reminded sportswriters that they underestimated the 1933 Buccaneers, and any good journalist surely must learn from his mistakes. Webb, while admitting to a suspect pitching staff, publicly expressed confidence that his team would once again surprise the Texas League. He praised Moody, Koehler and Sam Jack Evans for scouring the market for the best available players and assured the writers that his 1934 Bucs would again contend for the championship:

> *Show me a ballclub that outhustles their opponents and you have a first division club. That extra base on a hit or an error, that one man backing up his sidekick and advising him where to make the play, taking advantage of a rival pitcher's weakness to hold men on and several hidden acts on the field…are big factors in winning close ball games. Add to this mediocre ability and real team harmony, and you have a contender. I believe we have this sort of team in the making.*

The Buccaneers placed tremendous faith in four players received from Baltimore in exchange for Molesworth and Goldberg. Moose Clabaugh ranked among the finest batters in the minor leagues, Bob Linton brought experience at catcher and Don Robertshaw had shown potential at shortstop. Likewise, second baseman Hal King had been expected to fill the spot left vacant by Charlie English.

In the last week of training, Webb shelved many of his plans. English's return left Hal King out of a job, and Moose Clabaugh refused to report to Galveston, disgusted at being demoted from the more prestigious International League. After several tense days, Moody sold Clabaugh's contract to the Atlanta Crackers of the Southern League before he ever faced a Texas League pitch. Likewise, Webb decided to let Monty Stratton eventually develop at Baton Rouge after a few weeks with the Bucs. Jimmy Walkup, a veteran left hander, committed to replacing Stratton on the roster when Stratton left. Walkup brought versatility to the pitching staff, as he could start or serve in a relief role. Billy Webb, far from satisfied with the staff, had finally run out of time as the 1934 season was upon him.

April/May 1934

On April 17, Galveston opened the season at San Antonio, splitting a pair of games against the team that had defeating it in the 1933 championship series. Don Robertshaw committed the first of many early season errors, accounting for the losing margin in the season opener. A day later, Galveston's offense exploded for eighteen hits behind Harry Gumbert, including three from Buck Fausett, who also drove in four runs. With Wally Moses and Charlie English adding home runs, the Bucs claimed an easy 12–3 win, returning for their home opener with a 1-1 record.

On the nineteenth, Moody Stadium buzzed with opening day excitement as the Bucs prepared to host the Beaumont Exporters. A parade carried both teams from the Strand to the ballpark, and Guy Lombardo, in town for a performance at Sam Maceo's Hollywood Club, threw out the first pitch. Nearly six thousand fans witnessed a pitcher's duel, as Orville Jorgens allowed just two hits and struck out six Exporter batters in a 1–0 win.

One week into the season, *GDN* headlines focused on the positive (the outstanding Bucs offense) and the negative (the miserable play of shortstop Don Robertshaw). The struggling infielder accounted for six errors in the first seven games, including three in a 10–2 loss to Houston. The Buccaneer bats, on the other hand, picked up where they left off in 1933. Buck Fausett experienced the best start of his career, punching the ball through defensive holes at will, and Wally Moses pounded out extra-base hits on a daily basis. In the final game of the week, Beau Bell had his first of many impressive games to come, batting 4-4 and driving in four runs as Houston suffered a 19–11 whipping. The Bucs racked up twenty hits in the game, and Orville Jorgens claimed his second win on the young season. Billy Webb tempered any thoughts of overconfidence, noting that the Bucs could have won with batboy Walter Burns on the mound. After starting seven pitchers over the first seven games, though, Webb realized he had to settle on a pitching rotation. Monty Stratton and Glenn Liebhardt soon found themselves in the bullpen.

The early Texas League games led Bill Van Fleet to comment on how lively the ball appeared in the new season. Official scorers earned three dollars a game, and Van Fleet called for a pay increase if scores like 20–8 and 19–11 became routine. Roy Koehler took some of the credit for the Bucs' offensive outburst, claiming he purchased hickory rather than the less lively ashen bats. Van Fleet also heaped praise on Buck Fausett, claiming his arm to be the best in the Texas League, and noted that Beau

Bell's large hands and bat speed spelled trouble for opposing pitchers. Charlie English burst from the gate on a hot streak that Van Fleet wrote he couldn't possibly maintain.

During the season's second week, the Bucs' offensive attack continued, and the pitching of Hubbell, Hutchinson, Gibbs, Gumbert and Jorgens held opponents to four runs or fewer per game. Galveston took seven of its next eight, including a shutout and three games in which it allowed just one run. As the Bucs prepared for an early May fourteen-game northern road swing, they sat in first place, winning twelve of seventeen games. Charlie English led the team in batting with a .411 average, and Orville Jorgens and Harry Gumbert both held 3-0 records on the mound. Major-league scouts had already visited Galveston and expressed particular interest in Bell, English and Jorgens.

After Jorgens earned his fourth win in Fort Worth, the Bucs arrived in Tulsa for a series with the Oilers, who trailed Galveston by just one game in the standings. Playing in a park with no outfield fence, Tulsa erased the Buccaneers' advantage in just one afternoon, sweeping both games of a double-header to start the series. A day later, the Bucs carried a 9–3 lead into the final inning before Merritt Hubbell's pitching collapsed. Webb called Ira Hutchinson in as a reliever, but the Oilers came back and sent Galveston to its third straight loss. A day later, Joe Gibbs stopped the bleeding, pitching a five hitter as the Bucs scored six unearned runs in a 6–1 win.

Bill Van Fleet described the trip north as disastrous and noted that the Bucs' late inning collapses had destroyed the grocery business back on the island. After all, no one had the stomach for dinner after hearing the day's results.

While in Tulsa, Billy Webb made his first major roster move of the season, officially sending Monty Stratton to Baton Rouge and bringing Jimmy Walkup onto the roster. Walkup, a native of Havana, Arkansas, had major-league experience and, although aging, provided a stabilizing influence among the young pitching staff. His experience certainly might have been helpful a day later when shortstop Len Shires put Orville Jorgens on the edge of a five-game winning streak with a three-run home run in the top of the ninth inning against Oklahoma City. Reliever Ira Hutchinson couldn't hold the Indians in their half, however, and once again Galveston suffered a last-inning loss. When the rains arrived in Oklahoma on May 10, Billy Webb and his ball club breathed a sigh of relief and spent the off day mentally regrouping. The layoff helped, as the offense supported Harry Gumbert and Joe Gibbs with fourteen hits in a 10–4 win.

After the Bucs crossed back into Texas for a four-game series at Dallas, their pitching continued to falter. The Steers swept the series in impressive fashion, including a 7–6 win over Harry Gumbert, when Galveston granted Dallas six eighth-inning runs with four fielding errors. After two more road losses in San Antonio, the Bucs limped back to Galveston on May 15. With just three wins on the road trip, the small lead they had held in the standings two weeks earlier evaporated, their 15-15 record now only good for a fourth-place tie with San Antonio.

The Bucs' miserable performance on the road confirmed Billy Webb's fears about his pitching staff, which completed only three of eleven games. The offense, on the other hand, seemed unstoppable, having been held to a single run only twice and not suffering a shutout in the season's first thirty games. Despite the Bucs' drop in the standings, Webb received far worse news when catcher Jack Mealey suffered an injury in Oklahoma, keeping him off the field indefinitely.

With no one to replace Mealey on the roster, Webb prepared to activate himself for the Dallas series. Steer management, still angry about the Bucs' conduct in previous seasons, threatened to implement a seldom-enforced rule and require Webb to clear waivers before being activated. Dallas assured Shearn Moody it would claim Webb for the remainder of the season. The Steers' continued meddling with Galveston roster moves forced Webb to sign George Ham instead.

Billy Webb didn't rest on the Bucs' off day following the long road trip. Doctors broke the news that Mealey would be out for six weeks with a knee injury, the White Sox recalled Ira Hutchinson and Webb sent shortstop Don Robertshaw back to Baltimore, unable to stomach his piling stack of fielding errors. In Robertshaw's place, Webb temporarily signed local amateur Pookie Kirschner. In an effort to thwart another attempt by Dallas to disrupt the Bucs' operation, Webb placed himself on the suspended list based on "failure to remain in playing condition." Dallas squawked again, threatening to force a vote of league owners before he could be reactivated. President Gardner, apparently tired of Dallas's meddling, stated he would veto the vote regardless of the outcome. As Webb awaited Fort Worth's arrival for the first game of a well-deserved fourteen-game home stand, he traced each of the team's eleven road losses to a single play, allowing the floodgates to open on Buccaneer pitching. If those mistakes could be avoided, he believed his team could compete.

At home in Moody Stadium, the Bucs picked up their winning ways of two weeks earlier. In the opener against Fort Worth, they pounded out seventeen hits, including three each by Buck Fausett, Wally Moses, Tony Governor and Charlie English. Bob Linton topped off the offensive barrage with a grand slam en route to a 10–6 win. In all, the Bucs took five of the first six games on the home stand, Buck Fausett and Charlie English making a habit of three-hit games. Before leaving for Baton Rouge, Monty Stratton pitched a six-hitter in a loss to Tulsa. But as Stratton prepared for the train ride east, the White Sox called Shearn Moody and purchased the tall hurler's contract. After just two years in the low-level minors and a mediocre month in the Texas League, Stratton headed for the majors. He lasted only one game before being reassigned to Omaha of the Western League.

By the middle of the home stand, Galveston boosted its record to 20–17, just two games out of first place. Overall, the Texas League standings remained tight from top to bottom, with last-place Beaumont just three

A 1934 Buccaneers game-used baseball. *Courtesy of Rosenberg Library, Galveston, Texas.*

games behind fourth-place Dallas and playoff positioning. Galveston fans showed great interest in their team, but the Knothole Gang once again gave cause for grumbling.

The youngsters making up the Knothole Gang took their disrespectful fun to a new level, incessantly heckling opposing managers when introduced at each game's outset. Letter writers to the *GDN* complained that something needed to be done to teach the youngsters respect, and Bill Van Fleet agreed. "Opposing teams should be applauded during introductions," he wrote. "Bronx Cheers should be saved for the games." Little doubt, the Knothole Gang held plenty of "Galveston Jeers" in reserve.

With Monty Stratton having left the city and the Bucs short a pitcher, Billy Webb found a replacement in twenty-four-year-old Sigmund "Sig" Jakucki. Signed off the San Francisco sandlots, Jakucki displayed raw talent, having never played a professional game. At six-foot-three and two hundred pounds, the right-hander sought to overpower batters. Though he claimed to be Hawaiian, most questioned how a blond-haired, light-skinned fellow with a Polish name could be native to a Pacific Island. As it turned out, Jakucki never actually said he was a Hawaii native, but he did spend several years on the island while in the military. Sig was actually born in Camden, New Jersey, to Russian immigrants. As the season moved along, the big pitcher, regardless of where he called home, proved a valuable addition to the Bucs' rotation.

With Jack Mealey out of the lineup and Charlie English nursing a sore hamstring, the Bucs played .500 ball over the course of their long home stand. Despite Charlie English's four hits, Tulsa shut out Galveston for the first time in the season. Beau Bell and Charlie English home runs spotted Harry Gumbert a 9–3 lead in the series opener against Oklahoma City. Once again, Bucs pitching faltered in the late innings as reliever Joe Gibbs took a 10–9 loss. A day later, Jimmy Walkup made his first appearance of the season, pitching all fourteen innings until Tony Governor drove in new full-time shortstop, Len Shires, for a 4–3 victory. Unlike Robertshaw, Shires fielded the ball fairly well, but his batting served as a weak link in an otherwise powerful lineup. After Beau Bell's four hits and a home run combined with Charlie English to drive in six runs in an 8–6 win over the Indians, Webb announced the acquisition of shortstop Ray White from Indianapolis of the American Association. A mediocre batter, White offered a substantial upgrade over either Shires or Robertshaw defensively. Webb hoped fewer miscues at the shortstop position would encourage the rest of the infield to step up its game.

Galveston went on to lose two of its final three games of the home stand, with only Jimmy Walkup, among the oldest players in the Texas League at age thirty-six, saving the Bucs from a sweep at the hands of Beaumont. Batters claimed Walkup's arm to be so weak that their bats provided all of the power to drive the ball. But Walkup relied on deception. Over his first two starts, both victories, Walkup picked three runners off first base while striking out seven in twenty-three innings.

By taking two of three games from Galveston, Beaumont rose from last place to fifth in the standings. While Bill Van Fleet hoped an upcoming road trip would give the Bucs new life, he may have overstretched in comparing them to the mighty New York Yankees, who also found themselves in the middle of a late May slump. For its part, Galveston clung to fourth place, just a game and a half ahead of the Exporters.

June/July 1934

When the Bucs left Union Station on May 30, several fans expressed their displeasure with their performance to Bill Van Fleet, blaming both on-field and off-field issues. Complaints raged over the Knothole Gang, whose members were too busy getting free soda water to cheer on their team, as well as fair-weather fans who failed to encourage the Bucs when the scoreboard turned against them. But Wally Moses received the brunt of the criticism. Mired in a batting slump, Van Fleet reported that Moses had fallen into a "disconsolate mental state" over the hometown fans' lack of support. If nothing else, the road trip would give Moses a chance to get back on track without the pressure of the best and most knowledgeable fans in the Texas League.

Sig Jakucki made his first professional start in Houston on the road trip's second day, with disastrous results. The pitcher lasted less than an inning as the Buffaloes pounded out twenty base hits in a 16–5 romp. Six fielding errors contributed to Galveston's pitching miseries, and the Bucs had to call for the game's end after eight innings in order to a catch a train to San Antonio.

Before facing the Missions, Billy Webb and Roy Koehler made the first of two major roster moves, trading Merritt Hubble to Tulsa in return for Jim Bivin. A right-hander who preyed on right-handed batters, Bivin brought the Bucs his 5-3 record and 2.79 ERA. Billy Webb had witnessed Bivin's ability on the season's first road trip when he held the powerful Bucs lineup

Left: Acquiring pitcher Jim Bivin early in the season became a key to Galveston's 1934 success. *Author's collection.*

Below: Jim Bivin's autograph and a photo take from an autograph book. *Author's collection.*

to just three hits. Awaiting their new pitcher's arrival, the Bucs split the series with the Missions, committing three more errors in the opener as Harry Gumbert suffered a tough loss. The bats came alive for Orville Jorgens a day later when the lineup hit safely thirteen times, Buck Fausett's 3-5 afternoon leading them to a 6–3 victory. As the Bucs headed for Beaumont, Billy Webb celebrated what he finally considered a complete pitching staff with five legitimate starters on the roster.

Despite Jimmy Walkup continuing his unlikely string of victories with a four-hitter against the Exporters, negative fan mail continued to fill Bill Van

Fleet's inbox at the *GDN*. One writer complained that players no longer had to perform to get paid, as the elimination of bonuses for exceptional play destroyed all incentive for a ballplayer to give his best. Perhaps the writer received some encouragement in witnessing Jim Bivin's Galveston debut before the home crowd the following day.

While Ralph McAdams, a catcher on loan from Nashville, hit for the cycle, Beau Bell, Wally Moses and Roy White all added three hits each against San Antonio pitching. Jim Bivin pitched a near flawless game on the way to a 13–1 victory. The Missions found Bivin virtually unhittable, relying on bunts and the Bucs' suspect defense for its six base hits. Bivin's performance assured Billy Webb that, when backed by a powerful offense, he would be hard to beat. Still, with a loss the following day, the Bucs fell to fifth place and out of the playoff group for the first time all season. Another long northern road swing lay in wait.

While Buccaneer bats offered plenty of firepower, the team could not achieve offensive or defensive consistency. One day, Galveston bats would erupt and pitchers would completely shut down the opposition, but just twenty-four hours later, hitters might go silent and the pitching couldn't overcome the lack of run support. Harry Gumbert seemed the most frequent victim of poor offense, as the Bucs scored only twice in three of his losses. Meanwhile, Bill Van Fleet pointed out that former Buccaneer George Darrow faced a similar problem in the big leagues. Despite pitching a magnificent game against Carl Hubbell, Darrow's Athletics failed to record a run, and in another game against Brooklyn, Darrow again took a loss despite allowing only four hits.

The start of the Bucs' second long trip began as the first had ended, with Galveston winning only two of its first seven games. Although owning the Texas League batting leader Charlie English and a league-leading team average of .290, the Bucs simply couldn't string together hits when needed. Fortunately, Beau Bell couldn't have picked a better time to hit his stride.

With Bell's reputation growing throughout the minor leagues, big-league scouts followed the Bucs on their road trip, and Beau did not disappoint. Although he had earned the name "Pop Up" for his weak hitting as a rookie, over the course of three seasons in Galveston, Bell transformed into one of the league's most feared hitters, posting statistics similar to those he had at Texas A&M, when he became the university's first All-American athlete. By June 13, Bell's batting average had risen to .381, and his fifty-six hits included twenty-one doubles and seven home runs. When Galveston arrived in Oklahoma City, Beau Bell seemed able to hit the ball whenever and wherever he wanted.

With thirteen hits and two home runs in just four games, the big-league scouts couldn't help but take notice.

The end of the road trip in Oklahoma City proved to be just the tonic Billy Webb ordered. Jimmy Walkup, Orville Jorgens and Sig Jakucki pitched the Bucs to three straight wins, pulling the team above .500 after it had fallen to 29-30 on the year. Bell continued to impress with four hits and a home run in the series, and when the team left Oklahoma for a single game in Fort Worth, Billy Webb enthusiastically spoke of what lay ahead.

"In a race as close as we're having, anything can happen," he optimistically noted. "It doesn't look like there are any cripples against whom one club can fatten its percentage, but there'll end up being one good July club hard to beat out. So many teams can't keep up this torrid pace."

Slugging outfielder Beau Bell spent five seasons with Galveston before going on to the Major Leagues. *Author's collection.*

Despite his optimism, Billy Webb had to be disturbed at what happened to his pitching staff in Oklahoma City. Though sweeping the Indians, the Bucs suffered key injuries when Orville Jorgens and Harry Gumbert were hit by line drives in consecutive games. Jorgens appeared as if he would recover quickly, but Webb held doubts about Gumbert, who had taken a batted ball to his pitching hand. As a test, he chose to start Gumbert in Fort Worth. Gumbert pitched effectively, but the game ended in a 4–4 tie, prolonged by continuous arguing between new Cats manager Del Pratt and the umpiring crew. After Pratt disputed a decision to grant Galveston another at-bat before both teams had to catch trains, Galveston rallied to tie the score. When the Cats failed to score in their final half innings, the umpires ruled the game a tie, and police had to escort them from the ballpark. At the time, neither the umpires nor Buccaneer players knew how important the decision to allow the game to play on would become.

In the 1930s, long road trips followed by long home stands were the norm for Texas League teams. Economically, it made more sense to travel north for two weeks at a time to play Dallas, Fort Worth, Oklahoma City and Tulsa than it did to make multiple trips to play in only two cities. The southern franchises, particularly Galveston, Beaumont and Houston, required minimal travel, with San Antonio just a few hours' train ride away. A trip to the cities in North Texas and Oklahoma, on the other hand, exhausted a team both physically and mentally. With few off days scheduled, players could board a train at the end of one game and hope for a few hours of sleep on the way to the next city. At times, they would hardly be off the train before batting practice for the next game began.

The 1934 Galveston schedule included fourteen-, thirteen- and twelve-game road trips, sometimes ending with a series in one of the southern cities before the Bucs returned to Moody Stadium. Galveston's climate, as it had since Europeans first settled the island in the sixteenth century, sucked the life out of its residents, and baseball teams succumbed as well. From early July through the season's end, Galveston became an oven during the day and a sauna by evening. The heat, sun and humidity took a toll on both teams, but consistently playing in Galveston during the hottest part of the summer had historically proven to wear down the city's ball clubs. Winning games in April, May and June became particularly important, as performing at a high level became more difficult as the summer moved along. For the 1934 Buccaneers, their fast start in April, losing streak in May and inconsistent play through the first three weeks of June did not bode well for the remainder of the season. With the summer schedule about to bear down on the team, Billy Webb knew he needed to shake things up, and he and Roy Koehler prepared their second coup of the season.

When the Buccaneers returned from their second northern road trip, their 32-30 record left them in fifth place overall, one spot short of qualifying for the playoffs. With inconsistent pitching, when the offense clicked, the Bucs could outscore any team in the league. Too often over the first two months of the season, pitching had kept them in ballgames, but defense let them down. The loss of Keith Molesworth, despite his penchant for errors, left a void in the Buccaneer lineup—one that Billy Webb had yet to fill. He either needed a fielder or a hitter at shortstop, but preferably both. As his team prepared to play nineteen of its next twenty-four games at Moody Stadium, Webb worked the phones to sign Louisiana native Jim McLeod to serve as the Bucs' fourth starting shortstop that year. Roy White, a disappointment since his arrival in Galveston, left for his original team in Indianapolis.

Though born in Louisiana, McLeod moved to Little Rock, Arkansas, during his childhood. Growing up in a small house on what would eventually become the football field of Little Rock Central High School and headquarters for National Guard troops during the 1957 Little Rock Desegregation Crisis, McLeod's father simultaneously worked as a night watchman and carpenter. His work paid off, allowing Jim to attend the University of Little Rock from 1927 to 1930. There, he starred on the baseball team. At five-foot-ten and 160 pounds, McLeod offered fast feet and quick hands, something the Bucs lacked at shortstop all season. Sportswriters later noted Jim McLeod as an excellent fielder who would have been a major-league star had he had even moderate hitting ability. But in 1934, he provided an instant spark for Galveston and a desperately needed infield upgrade as the team prepared for the summer heat.

The Bucs began their home stand losing four of five games to Oklahoma City and Tulsa. Wally Moses continued his poor play, and the fans continued riding him. Whatever had gotten into his head earlier in the season had apparently returned, as Moses played miserably in his first four games at home. Bill Van Fleet no longer received negative mail about Moses; instead, the true Galveston fans urged support for the embattled outfielder. In the evenings, Wally became the object of as many hecklers as when playing on the road. During a 13–8 loss to Tulsa, Moses finally lost his temper, throwing his glove at a fan he believed had crossed the line. The outburst must have connected a missing circuit in Moses's game. The following day, Moses blasted out of his slump with a 3-5 performance, but the rest of the lineup offered little support, as Harry Gumbert fell again in a 4–2 loss. Galveston sat a game under .500, barely holding on to fifth place in the standings. With second-place Dallas and sixth- and seventh-place Fort Worth and Houston, respectively, coming to town for eight games, Billy Webb knew any chance the Bucs had to salvage the season hinged on the remainder of the home stand.

Galveston responded to the pressure in unprecedented fashion, as the pitching, offense and defense stepped up at the most opportune moments. First, the Bucs swept Dallas with Orville Jorgens, Joe Gibbs and Jim Bivin allowing just two runs in three games. Beau Bell and Charlie English carried the offense, driving just enough runs to overcome slumping outfielders Tony Governor and Buck Fausett. When Fort Worth arrived, Harry Gumbert continued the fine pitching, and Orville Jorgens turned in a second consecutive outstanding performance as the Bucs took the first two games. Had it not been for Fort Worth's need to catch a train, the Bucs may have swept the Panthers as well when, in the eighth inning of the finale, Buck

Fausett hit a tying home run. With the train waiting, the Cats had to give up the fight, leaving the teams deadlocked for the second time of the season.

Houston made the short trip to Galveston to wrap up the Bucs' home stand with a two-game series. In the first, Charlie English led the Bucs, batting 4-4 with a home run, while Jim Bivin allowed just two hits. Even more noticeable, the Bucs' defense received accolades for the first time all season as Jim McLeod turned in several outstanding plays in the field. A day later, Sig Jakucki took the mound and put forth his best performance of the season, allowing just four hits in a 14–0 shutout. Offensively, Galveston put on a clinic with English, Moses and Linton combining for ten hits, and McLeod proved he could contribute at the plate by driving in three runs. In the span of a week, the Bucs clawed their way back into fourth place while helping drop second-place Dallas to the lower half of the standings.

The season's first half came to a close with the Bucs dropping two of three against San Antonio, the series highlighted by a brawl between bench players Len Shires and San Antonio's Ash Hillin. League president J. Alvin Gardner observed a pair of the games and pointed out Jimmy McLeod as the apparent missing ingredient to Galveston's success. McLeod firmly plugged the gaping hole at shortstop, and Bell, Moses and English ranked second, third and fourth, respectively, in the race for the batting title.

After opening July with a win against the Missions, Jim Bivin took the mound against Beaumont on July 2 and turned in what Bill Van Fleet noted as the best pitching performance of the season. Though the Bucs managed just one run on returned catcher Jack Mealey's bottom of the ninth base hit scoring Tony Governor, Galveston claimed a 1–0 victory on Bivin's four-hitter. Tony Governor turned in the play of the game, firing a one-bounce strike to Mealey from deep center field, nailing a would-be Mission run at home plate. Jimmy McLeod's defense had apparently become contagious.

As Dallas lost sixteen of seventeen games, by July 9, Galveston sat alone in second place, trailing the league-leading Missions by just three games. The batting threesome of Bell, Moses and English remained red hot, with Bell hitting safely eight times while driving in ten runs over a four-game span. Nonetheless, an ongoing dispute between Jack Mealey and the umpires stole Bell's headlines.

Less than a year after umpires asked the police to forcibly remove Jack Mealey from the stadium during the 1933 championship series, the same crew had already ejected him twice in 1934. When the Bucs hosted Houston on July 3, the crew once again worked the game. While Beau Bell wowed the crowd with the longest home run Galveston had seen all season, the home plate umpire and Mealey consistently argued during the Bucs' 5–1 victory. The umpire normally put an end to squabbles by tossing the offending player, but on this evening Mealey snapped first, grabbing the umpire's facemask and dragging him to the ground. Bill Van Fleet observed the tension building throughout the game and wrote that the umpire did little to diffuse Mealey's growing anger. At one point, a fan begged Van Fleet to let him onto the field to stick up for the Bucs catcher. "They can't fine me," he argued. Perhaps the league wouldn't have fined him, but Galveston police probably would not have been so sympathetic. Several days later, J. Alvin Gardner fined Mealey and Billy Webb a combined thirty-five dollars for the incident. Fans backed their Buccaneers and tossed loose change in a pot to cover the penalty. All of Galveston seemed committed to supporting the Bucs, whether by threatening to charge the field in protest of poor umpiring or paying team fines. Even Sam Maceo jumped into the act, making up whatever shortage fans didn't cover for Mealey's and Webb's transgressions.

As the Bucs moved up in the standings, major-league scouts showed increased interest in the top players. Brooklyn actively sought to make a deal with Shearn Moody for Beau Bell, but Moody sat silent as other offers arrived. Bill Van Fleet wrote that he expected Moody to sell more players to big-league teams than any owner in recent memory, particularly if he followed Sam Jack Evans's pattern. Selling players would surely have disappointed the Bucs' number one fan, seven-year-old Betty Lou Kirschner, who sat directly behind the Bucs dugout every game encouraging the players and updating Bill Van Fleet on how former Bucs performed with their new teams. Some fans likely wondered why the Knothole Gang was not as well behaved and informed as little Betty Lou.

Following Jimmy Walkup's complete game 20–11 loss at Oklahoma City on July 14, Moody received an offer for Beau Bell he could not refuse. The St. Louis Browns agree to pay an unheard-of $17,500 for Bell's rights in 1935. Beau had taken the league lead in batting average, hits, doubles, home runs and runs, so the fact that the Browns eagerly signed him offered no surprise. The price tag, though, upped the ante for minor-league prospects around the country. Jimmy McLeod drew similar interest, his stellar play at shortstop having pulled the Bucs from the doldrums one month earlier.

For the Bucs, July brought plenty of activity both on and off the field. Aside from Jack Mealey attacking an umpire and Beau Bell commanding a hefty price, on July 10 Buck Fausett joined Shearn Moody as a new father when his wife, Anne, gave birth to a son, Robert Fausett Jr. The team presented Buck with a baby carriage as a gift, and he proceeded to push it around the bases and, to the delight of the fans, held on to the carriage as he slid into home plate. The carriage became an appropriate metaphor for what Fausett meant to the team, as he soon caught fire and carried the Bucs' offense over the course of several games. By July 20, Fausett had increased his batting seventeen points since his son's birth.

A day after Shearn Moody announced details of Beau Bell's sale to St. Louis, the Bucs received a blow when Joe Gibbs broke his collarbone in a collision with an Oklahoma City player. Earlier in the season, the injury may have devastated the Bucs' pitching staff, but Sig Jakucki had stepped up his game of late, at one point throwing fourteen consecutive scoreless innings. But after allowing just one run

Buck Fausett and his son Robert, circa 1940. *Courtesy of Robert J. Fausett.*

in three games against Beaumont, the pitching faltered against Oklahoma City, surrendering forty-four runs over a four-game span.

While injuries again plagued Galveston, Billy Webb experienced his worst two days of the season in Tulsa. First, he received word from Galveston that his car had been stolen, and the following day, a Tulsa teenage concession worker accused Webb of attacking him and had him arrested for assault. Though the young man admitted to heckling Webb and police found no marks on his body, a Tulsa judge still ordered that Webb stand trial on August 23. The 108-degree Tulsa heat, a stolen car and heckling from a punk employee of an opposing team apparently became too much for Webb to handle, and he agreed to return with the Bucs on their next trip to Tulsa to face trial. Fortunately, Galveston managed to take two of three games against the Oilers.

For all his troubles, Webb focused on baseball as the Bucs ended their northern road trip on a high note, taking three of four games at Fort Worth. As the Bucs rode the train home, they sat just one game behind league-leading San Antonio, the Missions due in Galveston for a crucial two-game series. On the trip south, Billy Webb declared the Bucs the most spirited team he had ever seen. Though the pitching staff had dwindled to five players, Joe Gibbs's injury healed quickly. Jimmy McLeod left the Bucs' early season shortstop troubles a distant memory, and many sportswriters considered him the premier Texas League shortstop. Further cheering Webb, Tulsa police notified him that all charges had been dropped after witnesses reported Webb had merely tried to detain the heckling teenager and deliver him to the Tulsa owner after he had been caught throwing a chair at Len Shires. With a massive baby shower planned for Buck and Anne Fausett at Moody Stadium, the stage seemed set for Galveston to seize control of the Texas League for the first time since early in the season.

While a second game rainout kept the Bucs from a shot at sole possession of first place, they pulled even with the Missions behind the deceivingly slow pitching of Jimmy Walkup. Buck Fausett thanked the fans for their barrage of baby gifts with a 3-5 performance, and Beau Bell hit another home run in a 4–2 Galveston win. With thirteen home games over the next two weeks, Galveston sat poised to leave the rest of the league behind.

While the Bucs concentrated on the pennant race, major-league scouts continued following the team wherever it traveled. Philadelphia's Athletics and Phillies both showed interest in several Buccaneers, as did the Baltimore Orioles. When Galveston swept a home series from Fort Worth, scouts saw little to diminish in any player's stock. Charlie English batted safely in six of his first seven at-

The 1934 opening day attendance trophy won by Galveston. *Bobby Moody Jr.*

bats in the series, including a home run, two RBIs and two runs scored. Buck Fausett went six for eight and turned in outstanding work in the field. Beau Bell continued playing hardcore baseball throughout the series, including one game in which he collided with defenders three times in trying to reach base. But the biggest surprise was Sig Jakucki, who, in a 7–5 win, gave the Bucs the winning margin with a two-run home run.

By the end of July, Moody Stadium ranked seventh out of eight ballparks in home runs allowed, with just twenty-eight balls sailing over the fences. Visiting clubs hit only nine of the four-baggers, and playing in Galveston made it all the more amazing that Beau Bell led the league in home runs. Even though fans loved offense, Moody Stadium had become the pride of Galveston, and fans were rewarded for their loyalty when J. Alvin Gardner presented Shearn Moody the trophy for the highest opening day attendance of any team in the Texas League. Moody vowed to donate $200 of the prize money to a local charity while drawing a lucky fan's name for $50 cash. The Moody family proudly displayed the silver chalice in their household as a testament to what the Galveston community could achieve when working toward a common cause.

AUGUST/SEPTEMBER 1934

When August arrived, the Bucs had won ten of twelve games, their pitching was flawless and their bats were as lively as at any point during season. Still, the team somehow trailed first-place San Antonio by three games. With the two teams scheduled to face each other seven times before the season's end, five times at Moody Stadium, fans and players alike had little doubt the season hinged on beating the Missions face to face.

Roster moves involving two teams in a league as small as the Texas League gave fans and executives alike a momentary pause. Fearing what might happen if the very player traded came back to bite them late in the season ranked high on the list of front office concerns. Except for shortstop, the Bucs' lineup remained relatively stable in 1934, despite a few players with nagging injuries. The front office shied away from trading with league opponents for most of the season, upgrading the roster by signing cast-offs from other leagues. Players like Ray White could simply be sent back from whence they came in 1930s minor-league baseball. As the season entered its final month, the only trade the Bucs made with a Texas League team remained the Merritt Hubbell–Jim Bivin exchange with Tulsa early in the season.

By August, few argued which team got the better end of the deal. Hubbell, though famous in name, lacked the talent of his brother Carl and had not pitched well since joining the Oilers. Jim Bivin, on the other hand, posted a 9-4 record for the Bucs, including two shutouts and four games in which he allowed only one run. Statistically, Bivin represented the difference in the two teams, as Tulsa trailed second-place Galveston by five games in the standings. Bivin knew he had to perform well in the final run for the pennant, and he disappointed himself in dropping his first appearance in August to his old team. Had he pulled out the win, it would have been a profound statement after the Bucs' 12–2 victory over Merritt Hubbell one night earlier.

When all appeared to be turning for the best, the first week of August saw the Bucs play their worst baseball of the season. At home against Oklahoma City and Tulsa and then on the road at Beaumont, Galveston won only two of seven games, scoring more than three runs only once. All the while, rumors swirled around the future of the Bucs' biggest stars.

With sportswriters not yet digesting the meaning of Beau Bell's $17,500 bid, the big leagues remained on the chase for Charlie English, Orville Jorgens, Jim Bivin and Wally Moses. In fact, by the end of the horrendous first week of August, Shearn Moody had sold both Jorgens and Bivin to the Phillies for cash, with the understanding that they would remain in Galveston until the Texas League season ended. Bill Van Fleet wrote that he expected the fire sale to continue. Sam Jack Evans's strategy had earned Moody a profit, and fans had little doubt that the Bucs' ability to turn minor leaguers into major-league talent would be enough to attract a new crop of talented players the following season.

With August 7 an off day, Van Fleet devoted his column to lamenting the recent slump, essentially throwing in the towel in the chase for first place. His concession may have been as much a mind game as anything, with the Bucs playing five of the next eight games against the league-leading Missions and only two and a half games separating the teams.

The Buccaneers kicked off one of the most important weeks of Galveston baseball since the nineteenth century when Jim Bivin tossed an 8–0 shutout at home against Beaumont, who saw its scoreless streak against Bivin extend twenty-nine consecutive innings. Bell, English and Moses all regained form, combining for five hits and five runs on the night. As the team prepared for its game the next day, it received another jolt when Shearn Moody announced the sale of Harry Gumbert to Baltimore. Bill Van Fleet noted that by season's end, Len Shires and batboy Walter Burns would be the only familiar faces in Moody Stadium. Shires corrected Van Fleet, announcing that he had sold himself for two cases of eggs and a crate of tomatoes. Regardless, the coming change of venue did not distract Gumbert, who pitched a six-hitter as Buck Fausett and Tony Governor led the Bucs to a 5–3 win.

After another win over Beaumont, the Bucs kicked off a five-game series with San Antonio. For their part, the Missions had eyes on essentially wrapping up the pennant over the course of the series, while the Bucs needed to win at least three of five to remain within striking distance. When all was said and done, Galveston achieved far more than it could have reasonably hoped.

Galveston pitching allowed the Missions just fourteen runs over the course of the series, while the Bucs' offense scored twenty-two. Fortunately, all of the bounces seemed to go Galveston's way, and by week's end the Bucs had swept the Missions, taking four of the five games by a single run, largely because of Jim McLeod's stellar play at shortstop, where he recorded thirty-nine putouts. Now deadlocked for first place, Galveston went on to win its next two games against Fort Worth, the second a fifteen-inning affair in which Jim Bivin went the distance and shut out the Panthers 5–0. Bivin's pitching performance rated as the best the Texas League had seen since 1920, an impressive post–dead ball era accomplishment. Galveston's nine-game winning streak not only erased San Antonio's lead in the standings, but it also padded the pitching staff's statistics. Galveston's staff made up five of the league's top thirteen pitchers, and the Buccaneers also ranked third in overall fielding and team hitting. The winning streak kept all of Galveston abuzz as "Dixie" blared over Moody Stadium's speakers during the seventh-inning stretch, and the Bucs left the field to "March of the Gladiators" after every win. Like the Gladiators, though, the Buccaneers soon proved themselves anything but invincible.

A 4–3 loss at Fort Worth broke the winning streak, as well as Charlie English's cheekbone. Hit in the face with a pitched ball, English lay unconscious for several minutes before rising and declaring himself ready to play ball. Instead, an ambulance rushed him to the hospital, where X-rays revealed a chipped cheekbone. Swelling caused English to miss the next five games, and the Bucs proved a different team with their second baseman out of the lineup.

With English sidelined, Galveston lost five consecutive games and began piling up errors during each. Harry Gumbert's pitching faltered, as he allowed a total of

The 1934 Texas League Most Valuable Player, Charlie English.
Author's collection.

twenty-eight runs in consecutive games against Dallas and Oklahoma City, the defense providing eleven errors to help the opponents' cause.

Bill Van Fleet saw a silver lining in the losing streak. If the Bucs' poor play without Charlie English did not prove he was the best all-around player in the league, nothing could. The only thing keeping English from being voted the Texas League's Most Valuable Player, Van Fleet believed, would be a split among sportswriters who credited both English and Beau Bell for carrying Galveston and settled on an alternative candidate.

For the 1934 Buccaneers, Jim Bivin served the role of slump-buster, and he did just that by striking out seven batters in a 4–3 win over Oklahoma

City. Still, the five losses dropped the Bucs three games behind San Antonio. When Harry Gumbert lost his third consecutive game the following day, chances of overtaking the Missions for first place appeared slim.

After losing six of seven games, the Bucs returned home and reversed course. Sig Jakucki pitched his team back into the win column with a 5–0 shutout of Tulsa, a game also marking the return of Charlie English to the lineup. As Charlie English went, so went the Buccaneers. They took three straight from Tulsa while allowing only one run. Joe Gibbs made his long-awaited return to the mound, dealing the Oilers a two-hit shutout in his first game back. But San Antonio kept winning as well, and the Bucs made no inroads on their three-game lead.

With Oklahoma City arriving in Galveston for a two-game series on August 27, the Bucs hoped to keep their streak alive, but Mother Nature had other plans. A tropical storm moving up the Gulf Coast swamped the island with seven inches of rain and tides three feet above normal. Though the power in Galveston went out for only a few hours and the top gale hit thirty-five knots, the conditions made Moody Stadium unplayable, and both the Bucs and Indians received two days of rest. The layoff did Galveston good as the team went on to win six of its next seven games, including shutouts pitched by Bivin, Walkup and Joe Gibbs. The only loss was a 1–0 affair to Fort Worth, and the Bucs outscored their opponents 34–6 over a ten-game stretch. The entire Buccaneer lineup followed the lead of Charlie English, who had batted .500 since his return. Buck Fausett, Wally Moses and Tony Governor joined English on his streak, and when August closed, Galveston trailed San Antonio by only one game.

Bill Van Fleet noted the pennant race might potentially end in controversy. Due to the Bucs' two tie games with Fort Worth, San Antonio had played more games than Galveston. If teams ended with the same number of wins, the Missions would fall a percentage point shy in the standings. Likewise, the Bucs could even claim the pennant with fewer wins than San Antonio but fewer losses as well. As the season entered its final week, the finish was anyone's guess.

The Bucs started the final push with a home series against Houston. After being rained out in the opener, they dropped both ends of a double-header the following day and fell two games behind the Missions. When San Antonio arrived in town a day later and topped Joe Gibbs 7–3, the Missions took a commanding three-game lead with just five remaining. Pitching in a must-win situation, veteran Jimmy Walkup came through for Galveston, riding Beau Bell, Charlie English and Joe Malay's barrage of extra-base hits to a 4–1 win, leaving them two games out of first place.

On September 7, the Missions headed to Beaumont to close out the season while Galveston traveled to Houston. The Missions seemed in complete control. Two wins against Beaumont or one win coupled with two Galveston losses would ensure San Antonio the Texas League pennant. Bill Van Fleet told the fans to get ready for a playoff series with Beaumont, as the odds of overtaking the Missions seemed slim at best.

Though awakening daily to must-win games, Shearn Moody did not give up on his new hobby of dealing players. The day before the Bucs left for Houston, he sold Buck Fausett and Charlie English to the Philadelphia Athletics. Between the A's and Phillies, Philadelphia would be home to seven members of the Buccaneers the following season. Before English hopped the train to San Antonio, Texas League sportswriters voted him MVP. He headed to Houston with a new ring and fifty dollars in cash for his efforts.

In Houston, the desperate Buccaneers refused to concede first place as Joe Malay's Texas League record–tying three triples led the offense to an 11–2 win in the series opener. But the victory became even more significant as word arrived from Beaumont that the Exporters had swept a double-header over the Missions. With Galveston and Houston scheduled for a double-header the following day, two Buccaneers wins coupled with another San Antonio loss would create the exact situation Bill Van Fleet had noted a week earlier.

The triples kept coming for the Buccaneers in the first game of the twin bill on September 8, with Joe Malay hitting his fourth in two games and Buck Fausett and Wally Moses adding one each. Jim Bivin pitched his sixth shutout on the season as they rolled to a 5–0 win and awaited results from Beaumont between games. The Exporters didn't disappoint. Though starting Paul Sullivan and his 3-9 record on his eighteenth birthday, the youngster threw his best game of the season, matching Bivin with a 5–0 shutout. With San Antonio having lost three consecutive games, the Bucs headed into the nightcap only needing a win to secure the Texas League pennant for the first time since 1899.

In the second game against Houston, the Bucs came together for a rare complete game. Charlie English and Tony Governor's timely hitting and Jim McLeod's stellar defense backed Orville Jorgens's pitching in a 7–1 victory. With the win, the Bucs were guaranteed a first-place finish regardless of the outcome of the season finale.

Thirty-four years to the day after the Great Storm of 1900 devastated Galveston, the Buccaneers brought Galveston the pennant it had awaited since the year before the hurricane seemingly destroyed the city's future.

With nothing on the line, Galveston didn't offer much competition in the season finale. Third base coach Len Shires played every position except right field, and seldom-used pitcher Hoke Garcia went the distance in an 11–1 loss. Despite a San Antonio win leaving them with a final record of 89-65, Galveston's 88-64 finish topped the Missions by 1/100 of a percentage point. The tie games with Fort Worth proved among the most important of the season, as did every other victory, whether coming in April or August. For the second consecutive season, Galveston faced Dallas in the playoffs first round, with San Antonio taking on third-place Beaumont.

Though the Missions had vetoed Galveston's request to replace injured pitcher Euel Moore on its playoff roster a year earlier, when San Antonio's player-manager Hank Severeid suffered an injury in the season's final series, Roy Koehler had no intention of preventing his replacement. Shearn Moody, on the other hand, objected to the move. Moody ordered Koehler to vote against the roster change, not because he held a grudge over the previous season, but because he believed his team owed Beaumont for setting the stage and allowing Galveston to win the pennant.

Immediately after Galveston sewed up first place, a coin toss decided whether the Bucs or Steers would set the schedule for the five-game series. Galveston won the toss, and Roy Koehler chose to risk allowing Dallas three home games to end the series in exchange for playing the opening two at Moody Stadium. Despite the Steers finishing eight and a half games behind Galveston, the teams split their twenty-two regular season games, and Koehler knew winning early in the series was more important than playing Game 5 at home. In fact, he bet on the series never reaching a deciding game.

When the Kiwanis Club honored the Bucs for their pennant, Billy Webb gave his players all the credit and accepted none. "They won the ballgames because they were the best club," he said. "My share of the work was along the organizational line. They made the base hits and did the pitching."

Beau Bell showed up at the Kiwanis event sporting a new suit. "I bought it with the championship money, and I'd like to get another with the Dixie Series profits," he announced.

But batboy Walter Burns stole the show that evening with his short response to a club member's question. "I think it'll be a breeze to win the Dixie Series," he said. The team then handed out souvenir cards printed with a triangle and the words "Galveston Buccaneers, 1934 Pennant Winners."

FIRST-ROUND PLAYOFF, 1934

The playoff schedule allowed Galveston and Dallas two off days before the series began on September 12. In the meantime, fans lined up at Moody Stadium for tickets, paying one dollar for the best seats in the house and as little as a quarter to watch from the bleachers.

On September 11, Billy Webb announced twenty-game winner Jim Bivin would pitch the series opener. Harry Gumbert and Joe Gibbs each posted 3-1 records against Dallas, but Bivin's six shutouts and late-season heroics made him a logical choice to sew up an all-important Game 1 win. The following day, it quickly became obvious that Game 1 would be postponed as a steady rain soaked Moody Stadium. The rainout offered a bit of a blessing for Galveston, as Joe Malay and Buck Fausett had both been nursing colds. By the time the two teams arrived at the ballpark on the thirteenth, Billy Webb had juggled his pitching rotation and started Harry Gumbert, who had shut out the Steers earlier in the season.

With 5,045 fans watching from the stands, Harry Gumbert baffled Steers batters all evening. Pitching a five hitter, he bested Dallas in a 4–1 victory. Offensively, Beau Bell starred for the Bucs, batting 3-4 with two runs and a double. Tony Governor and Jim McLeod each added a pair of hits and RBIs to account for all four Galveston runs. But like most matchups with Dallas, the game offered its share of controversy. *Dallas Journal* sportswriter Flinte Dupre traded barbs with Bill Van Fleet over Beau Bell's choice to sit out the final game against Houston, his only chance of winning the batting title being if Tulsa's Alex Hooks failed to get a hit. Likewise, Dallas's Joe Vance became involved in a heated argument with umpire Steve Basil, who at one point appeared ready to engage Vance in fisticuffs. Instead, he simply tossed the hotheaded Vance from the game.

For Game 2, Billy Webb took a risk in choosing Jimmy Walkup to pitch, his one win against Dallas that season being a shutout. Based on the difficulty Dallas batters had against Gumbert's slow curveball, Webb seemed confident that Walkup's off-speed pitching would keep them off balance. Webb made a masterful choice, as the 4,028 in attendance saw Walkup scatter seven hits and strike out four in a 6–3 win. Bob Linton led the way offensively, batting 2-4 with three RBIs, while Jim McLeod batted in two runs.

Roy Koehler breathed a sigh of relief as Galveston took a 2-0 series lead to Dallas. His risk in choosing to play the three final games on the road would be

Despite his age and weakening arm, veteran pitcher Jimmy Walkup baffled opposing batters all season with his off-speed delivery.

successful only if the Bucs took both games at Moody Stadium and his confidence proved fruitful. The Bucs boarded the train for Dallas needing just one win, with Jim Bivin scheduled to start the following evening.

Dallas fans waited game time in rabid anticipation. The 10,582 in attendance saw an outstanding ballgame, as the teams entered the ninth inning tied 2–2. Wally Moses, Beau Bell and Bob Linton's combined four hits provided all of Galveston's offense, and when the Bucs failed to score in the top of ninth, Jim Bivin prepared to face outfielder Stan Shino to lead off the Dallas half of the inning. Though Shino played only forty-eight games on the season, he hit seven home runs and had added another earlier in the game against Bivin. With over 10,000 fans screaming their approval, Shino led off the bottom of the ninth with his second home run of the game, giving the Steers a 3–2 win over the Bucs' ace pitcher. With his heroics, Shino single-handedly gave the Steers a chance to tie the series less than twenty-four hours later against Harry Gumbert.

Before a hostile crowd of twelve thousand, Gumbert faced a determined Dallas team in Game 4, and the Bucs aided them with three fielding errors. Gumbert, though, allowed only six hits, and Dallas strung enough together to score only two runs. All Buccaneer scoring came in the fourth inning when they hit four consecutive doubles, including one by Orville Jorgens, who had batted .073 that season. Ironically, as Jorgens strolled to the plate, the notoriously slow Jimmy Walkup jokingly shouted, "You're the one hitter I'll always be able to outslug!" As Jorgens dusted himself off at second base, Walkup giggled heartily in the dugout. The barrage of doubles and a base hit from Buck Fausett led to all five Galveston runs. They cruised behind Gumbert's pitching for the remainder of the game, posting a 5-2 victory and a 3-1 series win. Knocking Dallas from the playoffs for the second year in a row earned the Bucs a Texas League Championship series rematch with San Antonio, which had won the final two games against Beaumont to claim a 3-2 series win.

Dallas reacted to the Galveston victory as it had to most everything else the Bucs accomplished over the previous two seasons. Only one Steer player crossed the field to offer congratulations. Bill Van Fleet noted that when the Bucs dropped the championship series to San Antonio the previous season, Shearn Moody, Billy Webb and Roy Koehler had met the Missions in their clubhouse to offer congratulations. With or without Dallas's well wishes, the Galveston Buccaneers left on a train bound for the Texas League Championship series for the second straight season.

THE 1934 TEXAS LEAGUE CHAMPIONSHIP SERIES

Over the course of the Dallas series, Galveston's pitching allowed just five earned runs, aided by stellar defense and Steer base runners afraid to test Tony Governor's center field arm. The Bucs entered the championship series healthy, although Wally Moses and Jim McLeod both spoke of minor injuries.

The Texas League championship was a seven-game affair, the first two at San Antonio, followed by three at Galveston and then a coin flip to determine where the final two games, if needed, would be played. With a two-day layoff, Billy Webb chose to again send Harry Gumbert to the mound in Game 1, even though he had pitched two games against Dallas. Webb's playoff strategy continued to pay dividends.

With an overflow crowd of 9,200 packing Tech Field, Galveston fans crowded around radios on the island listening to the San Antonio broadcast, while many ladies kept themselves busy, too nervous to follow the game. Before a hostile crowd, the Bucs pounded out sixteen hits on the night, scoring six runs in the eighth inning. Every Buccaneer batter hit safely, with Charlie English and Wally Moses gathering three each. In the decisive eighth inning, Harry Gumbert helped his own cause with a two-run single, slamming the door on the Missions in an 8–3 victory.

For Game 2, Billy Webb took a less conventional gamble in placing Sig Jakucki on the mound. Though Sig went 10-7 for the Bucs, he hadn't pitched in sixteen days, and the rust appeared from the game's first pitch. Jakucki faced four batters to start off the game, walking two and hitting two with pitches. Rather than risk further damage, Webb brought on Joe Gibbs in

Front row—Sam Harshany, Charles Engle, Arthur Scharein, Geo. W. Stanton, Everett Purdy, Connally. Row 2—Schuhart (Mascot), Chester C. Morgan, Payton, Thomas Heath, Larry J. Bettencourt, Faz (Mascot). Back row—Harold Wiltse, Earl Caldwell, A. R. Miller, Henry Severeid (Mgr.), Howard R. Mills, H. Ashley Hillin, Geo. A. Mills.

SAN ANTONIO CLUB—RUNNERS-UP IN TEXAS LEAGUE PLAY-OFF.

The 1934 San Antonio Missions. *Author's collection.*

relief. Despite four extra-base hits, including a triple from Gibbs, the Bucs saw their fate sealed in the fifth inning when San Antonio scored five runs. Along with Jakucki's first-inning disaster, the Bucs' defense recorded three errors in a 7–3 loss in front of seven thousand fans.

Rather than dwell on the loss, Bill Van Fleet chose to write about the miseries of rooming with Sam Jack Evans. The sportswriter wrote of the telephone ringing incessantly at all hours of the night as fans called to check in on their baseball heroes. The only advantage to rooming with Evans, he wrote, was the ability to make long-distance phone calls at no charge, as Shearn Moody would simply assume Evans had placed them. After just two nights, Van Fleet understood why players considered Evans the team's worst roommate; in fact, by season's end, a player rooming with Evans could place him on waivers, offering a replacement seven cents for another bed. Roommates seldom found buyers.

The return to spacious Moody Stadium offered a relief to the Bucs, if not J. Alvin Gardner himself. The overcrowded Tech Field in San Antonio had resulted in the loss of eighty baseballs over the first two games. At a cost of $1.50 each, Gardner feared many more would bankrupt the league. But the crowds in Galveston didn't rival those in Dallas or San Antonio, and only three thousand turned out to watch Jim Bivin pitch Game 3. Perhaps the rest ran late and realized after the first inning that the Bucs had the game in the bag.

After Bivin retired San Antonio in the top of the first inning, the Bucs put the game away before the Missions got back to the plate. Following Joe Malay's foul ball out, eight consecutive Galveston batters hit safely, highlighted by Tony Governor's inside-the-park home run, a hit that would have surely been a ground rule double in San Antonio. Jim Bivin had all the support he needed as the Bucs cruised to a 7-2 win and 2-1 series lead.

The following night, Jimmy Walkup took the mound and confounded San Antonio batters. Wally Moses, Buck Fausett and Joe Malay had two hits each, and Walkup joined them in support of his cause with two of his own. But with two outs in the bottom of the ninth and Walkup clinging to a 3–2 lead, Webb reached for the bullpen when the Missions' tying run reached third base. Harry Gumbert threw one pitch to force the final out, and Galveston's 3-1 series lead placed it on the verge of a Texas League Championship.

Despite a crowd of five thousand, Orville Jorgens's four-hitter and the Buccaneers' eleven base hits, somehow San Antonio managed to slip off Moody Stadium's field with a 4–0 shutout in Game 5. The deeply disappointed Buccaneers saw matters go from bad to worse when Roy

The 1934 Galveston Buccaneers, Texas League champions. *Courtesy of Robert J. Fausett.*

Koehler lost the post-game coin flip, sending the series to San Antonio for the final two games.

Tech Field expected another overflow crowd, and Galveston feared that the fans' ability to interfere with the game, willingly or unwillingly, could cost them the series. Billy Webb sent Harry Gumbert, his most reliable pitcher of late, to shut down the Missions' dreams of a comeback. With three playoff wins to his credit and clinching a Game 4 win, Webb believed Gumbert to be money on the table. It didn't take long to learn if he bet correctly.

For the second time in three games, the Bucs scored all the runs they needed in the first inning. Stalwarts Beau Bell, Buck Fausett and Wally Moses punctuated their outstanding seasons with two hits each. Tony Governor gathered three of his own, and Charlie English justified his Texas League MVP award with four hits, including a double and two RBIs. Gumbert allowed only two runs on the evening, and by the time Beau Bell slammed a two-run homer in the eighth, the series was all but decided. Galveston claimed the Texas League Championship with a 9–2 victory and a 4–2 series win.

The Dixie Series lay in wait, but first a celebration awaited Galveston at the Buccaneer Hotel. In the wee hours of the morning, the Bucs boarded a train for home in what would surely be the shortest ride of the season.

THE DIXIE SERIES

The break between the Texas League Championship and the Dixie Series provided the Bucs with one day to celebrate. Fortunately, the series began in Galveston, so the still jubilant team didn't have to reboard the train for a 350-mile trip to New Orleans. But even in friendly Moody Stadium, Billy Webb and his team knew they would have to be on top of their game to defeat the Pelicans. New Orleans came to Galveston to defend its Dixie League Championship over San Antonio a year earlier. Its loyal fan base invested time and money following the Pelicans on the road, and the Bucs expected a healthy contingent of New Orleans rooters on hand. Most formidably, New Orleans stacked its lineup with some of the best minor leaguers of the day; in fact, of the eighteen players on the Pelicans' 1934

Beau Bell's 1934 Texas League Championship ring. *Dianne Sides, Mary Mowlam, Doug Suhr and Rosenberg Library, Galveston, Texas.*

roster, fifteen eventually played in the Major Leagues, including the entire pitching staff. With ninety-four wins on the season, New Orleans took the Southern Association pennant handily over second-place Nashville and then beat the Volunteers 3–2 for the championship.

Four of the five Pelican pitchers won at least twelve games in 1934, with twenty-year-old Al Milnar finishing the season with a 22-13 record, followed closely by Fred Johnson at 20-5. But the staff did have its weaknesses. Only Milnar finished the season with an ERA below 3.00, and the three staff members included a thirty-six- and forty-year-old pitcher. The Pelicans didn't offer nearly as potent an offense as Galveston. Pitcher Clay Bryant led the team with a .327 batting average, with Boze Berger's .314 the best among everyday players. The Pelicans hit just fifty-nine home runs on the season, but what they lacked in power they made up for in speed. With 262 doubles and 77 triples, Pelican batters threatened to turn any routine single into extra bases. Defensively, New Orleans excelled and bailed out its pitchers on several occasions. With strong support behind them, not a single Pelican pitcher posted a losing record.

The Booster Boys Band welcomed the Pelicans' arrival at Union Station along with a sizeable group of Galveston's well-wishers. The Pelicans then headed to Moody Stadium while Billy Webb mulled his approach for the opening game. Jim Bivin ultimately got the nod for the Bucs, while New Orleans manager Larry Gilbert started sixteen-game-winner Clay Bryant. The pitchers dueled for nine innings, and when three Buccaneers batters reached base in the bottom of the ninth, it appeared Galveston would beat Clay Bryant in Game 1. But Bryant and the Pelican defense responded, sending the 2–2 game into extra innings. As Larry Gilbert had hoped, Bryant drove in the winning run with a twelve-inning double. Jim Bivin took the tough loss in front of 4,700 fans. Billy Webb's attempt to reach back to the bunting drills from spring training in each of the final two innings failed, as the outstanding Pelican defense turned both into double plays.

With only two thousand in attendance, Jimmy Walkup took the mound for Game 2, allowing just four Pelican hits. New Orleans boosted the Galveston offense by committing four errors, as Charlie English led the Bucs with a 3-4 night at the plate. After tying the series with an easy 8–1 win, the teams prepared for the all-important Game 3, the Bucs' last home game of the year.

Orville Jorgens started Game 3, and to say it wasn't Jorgens's best outing of the season would be an understatement. The Pelicans chased Orville early, and Galveston's pitching allowed nine hits on the night, with another

"The Eyes of Texas Are Upon You"

BUCCANEERS!

LET'S WIN THE DIXIE SERIES OF 1934

BUCS: The "Eyes of Texas" are looking to you to bring the Dixie series trophy to Galveston. Texans believe you're just the club to do the job . . . and Galvestonians know you are.

We're backing you, Billy Webb and your baseball troupers 100%. We believe you can finish out in front—with something to spare. You're that kind of a club. So, let's go, Buccaneers!

THE FOLLOWING LOYAL GALVESTON FIRMS ARE 100% BEHIND YOU:

City National Bank
"Galveston's Most Progressive Banking Institution"

American National Insurance Co.
Home Office, Galveston, Texas

E. S. Levy & Co.
"Reliability Since 1877"

McBride's
Department Store

Kahn & Levy
Phone 3403   2117 Church St.

Madden's Furniture Co., Inc.
Phone 484   2017 Ave. E.

Robt. I. Cohen
Market Street

Sui Jen

Interurban-Queen Cigar Stand
Market at 21st   (Old Witherspoon Corner)   Phone 2008

Model Dairy
24th and G   Phone 6122

Businesses throughout Galveston offered their support to the Buccaneers as they headed for the Dixie Series against New Orleans in 1934. *Galveston Daily News.*

twelve runners reaching base on eleven walks and an error. The Bucs' offense narrowly avoided a shutout by scoring two runs with two outs in the bottom of the ninth inning. The Pelicans took a 9–2 win and a 2-1 series lead into the travel day to New Orleans.

Despite trailing by only one game, the Game 3 loss placed the Bucs in a major hole, having to win three of four games in hostile Pelican Park. Billy Webb called on Jim Bivin again in Game 4, but the Pelicans scored eight runs on twelve hits while Galveston's offense provided little support in an 8–0 loss. With the season on the line, Webb gambled again, sending Bivin back to the mound for Game 5. This time, the early season acquisition delivered.

Although Bivin allowed nine runs on fifteen hits, the Bucs played their best offensive game of the series, chasing Clay Bryant before he finished the first inning. Charlie English's four hits led a fifteen-hit attack, including English's three-run triple and six RBIs. With the 11–9 win, the offense appeared to have come alive at just the right moment. As the teams prepared for Game 6, Billy Webb rolled the dice with his inconsistent pitching staff, Jimmy Walkup earning the call.

In what probably ranked as the series' best game, Walkup allowed fourteen hits but scattered them in holding the Pelicans to five runs, with the Galveston defense contributing two vital errors. Buccaneers batters gathered nine hits, with Buck Fausett accounting for three while Bob Linton added a triple and three RBIs. With Galveston trailing 5–4 heading into the ninth inning, Joe Malay led off with a single, but the Pelican defense again snuffed out Buck Fausett's effort to sacrifice him into scoring position. Beau Bell followed with a strikeout, and the Bucs' season came down to Wally Moses. Though the embattled outfielder had come through in the pinch many times over the course of the season, Moses softly grounded out, giving the Pelicans a 5–4 win and their second consecutive Dixie League Series.

Inconsistent batting and pitching bit Galveston against New Orleans. The Bucs didn't put together a complete game in the series, as either the offense, defense or pitching failed to show up each night. With the exception of Charlie English, no Buccaneer played particularly well during the series. Galveston gathered hits in spurts, as opposed to the Pelicans hitting safely in bunches.

Regardless of the outcome of the Dixie Series, the 1934 Galveston Buccaneers achieved what had seemed an impossible goal: winning the Texas League Championship with, arguably, the best ball club Galveston had ever seen. Though the $145 share each player received for the postseason was a disappointment, neither team had drawn well in the Dixie

Series. Galveston fans still celebrated their Texas League crown throughout the series, with the Pelican crowd maybe a bit conceited after a second long, successful season.

Upon arriving in Galveston, Buccaneers players quickly scattered, with seven heading north to join their new big-league franchises, but Buck Fausett remained on the island until spring training began in Cincinnati. Fausett had come a long way in two seasons. Aside from joining Shearn Moody as a married man and father, he had developed into a well-rounded ballplayer. Though Buck's batting average dropped from a high of .323 in 1933, his fielding improved dramatically as he turned in 336 assists and nearly 200 put outs. Likewise, Fausett added power and speed to his game, hitting the first four home runs of his career and tying for the team lead with fifteen triples. Combined with an increasing number of stolen bases and playing in every Buccaneers game of the season, Fausett had transformed into the ballplayer Billy Webb and Shearn Moody hoped he would. At just twenty-six, Buck Fausett's career appeared set to blossom.

For Shearn Moody's part, he made a healthy profit dealing players and brought a championship trophy home in the process. When Billy Webb requested a bonus, though, Moody refused. After all, Moody was a businessman, and Webb's contract had no provision for a bonus. Webb soon resigned his position for a coaching slot with the White Sox. Moody didn't have to look far for his replacement, signing Jack Mealey to manage the 1935 club just two weeks later.

9

DECLINING DREAMS AND DEVASTATING LOSSES

Shearn Moody and Jack Mealey both realized duplicating the 1934 Buccaneers' success would be no easy task. With eight starting pitchers and position players having left for the majors or other leagues, the front office faced a challenge finding replacements. Sig Jakucki and Tony Governor planned to return, as did Jim McLeod, but the pitching staff required an overhaul. Likewise, the loss of Beau Bell's league-leading 348 total bases, 157 extra-base hits and 51 doubles would create a serious hole in the batting lineup.

Jack Mealey brought fourteen years of professional baseball experience to his management position. A proven winner, Mealey had played on seven pennant-winning teams in his career and never experienced a losing season. A career-long catcher, Mealey's leadership experience had been boosted when serving as Billy Webb's right-hand man over the previous two seasons. Bill Van Fleet wrote that Mealey would give the fans what they wanted: "a clean, hard-fighting, hustling team that never gives up until the game is over."

Both Moody and Jack Mealey received a pre-season surprise when the White Sox again optioned Charlie English back to Galveston. Apparently an MVP honor and consecutive outstanding seasons didn't convince the Sox that English had major-league potential. The Bucs caught another break when Buck Fausett returned, albeit under extremely different circumstances.

Buck Fausett valued loyalty, whether that meant working on the family farm, attending East Texas Teachers College or playing professional

After thirteen minor-league seasons, Buck Fausett made his major-league debut as a thirty-six-year-old rookie in 1944. *Courtesy of Robert J. Fausett.*

baseball. Shearn Moody had shown Fausett that type of loyalty, not only in giving him his first real shot at professional baseball, but also by employing him in the off-season. Fausett met his wife in Galveston, the couple had their son on the island and he enjoyed playing for the Buccaneers. The big leagues enticed any ballplayer, but Buck wasn't going to leave for just any deal. During training camp with Philadelphia, manager Connie Mack called Buck into the office and presented a contract. Major League Baseball had called, almost guaranteeing him a permanent ticket away from life as a farmer. Buck Fausett's dream was on the desk, requiring just a signature to be fulfilled. At the same time, though, Galveston seemed to be calling him home.

As Buck looked over the terms of the contract, he questioned the salary the future Hall of Fame manager offered. Quickly running the calculations in his head, Buck then informed Connie Mack that he could make more money in Galveston. Buck's bold reply caught Connie Mack off guard. After all, how could a minor-league club offer a contract rivaling that of a big-league team in a city hosting two franchises? Buck explained his off-season arrangement with Shearn Moody and noted that he had no guarantee of off-season employment in Philadelphia. After a brief discussion, Fausett left Connie Mack's office without a contract in hand, soon calling Roy Koehler and Shearn Moody to see if they still needed a third baseman. Shearn Moody eagerly accepted him back, as did Jack Mealey. And Moody couldn't have been more impressed with Buck's loyalty. With Fausett and English in the lineup, the Bucs might stand a fighting chance after all.

Right: Max Butcher's twenty-four wins led the 1935 Bucs to their third consecutive Texas League playoff berth. *Author's collection.*

Below: Harry Gumbert's baseball-themed gravestone, Wimberly, Texas. *Karen Rutherford.*

Over the course of 1935, Charlie English continued to put up big numbers, but Fausett's batting average fell to just .258. His fielding held steady, and with Sig Jakucki developing into a fifteen-game winner, Max Butcher leading the club with twenty-four victories and Ed Cole pitching the first perfect game in Texas League history, Galveston managed a third-place finish, nine games behind the league-leading Oklahoma City Indians. Under another year of the Shaughnessy Plan, the Bucs faced Beaumont in the playoffs. After taking the first two games, Galveston succumbed to the Exporters in the final three, thus ending their run at a second consecutive championship.

At season's end, Shearn Moody again cashed in, selling Max Butcher to the Brooklyn Dodgers and once again earning a profit on Charlie English's rights in a sale to the New York Giants. English never converted his minor-league success to the major-league level, and after two brief stints with the Giants, he went on to an eighteen-year minor-league career. Indianapolis of the American Association called Buck Fausett, and he spent five years in the league before moving on to Little Rock and the West Coast in player-manager positions.

Jack Mealey made plans to return for 1936, but he first had to convince Shearn Moody that selling good ballplayers was not the only way to profit from baseball. Galveston fans turned out for three consecutive winning seasons despite Moody selling the team's stars each year. Mealey wasn't sure the Bucs could continue to acquire talent on the level of Beau Bell, Buck Fausett, Charlie English and Wally Moses, and pitchers like Harry Gumbert and Max Butcher were few and far between. Moody relented, vowing he was in the Texas League for the long haul. After all, in July 1935, he had become a father for the second time, as Frances gave birth to Robert Lee Moody. With two children, perhaps Shearn had mellowed and concluded that building wealth wasn't the only way to become successful. He had already left a mark on the Texas League and intended to bring more championship trophies to Galveston. Little did his manager, front office, father or wife and children realize, but the dashing, athletic businessman would not see spring training.

Despite the 1,100 miles separating Galveston and Chicago, Illinois, the two cities had much in common. Both incorporated in the 1830s based on economic geography and westward expansion. By the end of the nineteenth century, both had grown into financial centers on national and international stages. As the population became more mobile, both cities became tourist destinations and remained home to some of America's most wealthy citizens. Of course, Chicago's population of 3.3 million dwarfed Galveston's 55,000 residents; then again, Chicago didn't face the boundaries of being surrounded by the sea.

Even though Chicago lacked the ocean access Galveston enjoyed, it did sit on the southern shore of Lake Michigan. While it lacked a natural harbor, the Chicago River offered protection from the often-stormy waters of the Great Lakes, just as the island protected the port of Galveston. When the Erie Canal connected the Great Lakes to the Atlantic Ocean in the 1820s, business interests searched for a shipping center on the west end of the region, and Chicago fit the bill. Chicago, like Galveston, became a major regional port of trade, providing dry goods and other imports to sustain an exponentially growing population while exporting agricultural products and resources grown in nearby states. The railroads contributed greatly to both cities' development, with the ability to quickly transport commodities from inland communities to water-based ports rapidly growing the economy of each. While W.L. Moody and Company created its fortune through transporting raw materials from inland Texas to Galveston, Richard Sears and Aaron Montgomery Ward did just the opposite, obtaining dry goods by import and selling them via mail order to points inland.

By the 1930s, Galveston and Chicago also shared the problem of organized crime. Just as Sam Maceo had built his family's control of the Galveston underworld of gambling houses, brothels and "speakeasies" during Prohibition, renowned gangsters Al Capone, Dion O'Banion and Bugs Moran held firm control over Chicago crime. Although Chicago gangsters brought the city much more violence and notoriety than the Maceos brought Galveston, both profited from Prohibition and turned their respective cities into entertainment meccas by opening nightclubs attracting big-name musicians. The Chicago police and FBI fought a war with their gangsters, while the Maceos lived in relative peace as local and state law enforcement generally turned their heads.

Along with similarities in terms of development, economics and crime, Chicago and Galveston had something else in common: disasters, either natural or man-made. Galveston endured many disease outbreaks, as did Chicago, its unsanitary living and working conditions breeding sites for epidemics. Likewise, a natural disaster nearly wiped Galveston from the map in 1900, and many Chicagoans suffered similar fates in 1871, when

Shearn, W.L. Moody Jr. and William Moody III in December 1936. This is the last-known photograph of the Moody men together before Shearn's death just two months later. *Courtesy of E. Douglas McLeod/Moody Archives.*

a nearly four-square-mile area of its business district burned. The resulting three hundred deaths and loss of eighteen thousand structures left well over one-third of the city's population homeless. And like Galveston in 1900, strong winds fueled much of the disaster, spreading the fire throughout the city faster than firefighters could respond.

With so much in common, it is not surprising that Galveston and Chicago had business connections. From port policy to banking to printing, business leaders shared many common interests and often consulted on matters of governmental policy. In February 1936, following a trip to New York City, Shearn Moody arrived in Chicago to discuss some of these interests with local business leaders.

When Moody left Galveston around February 10, the island experienced an abnormal heat wave, even for its subtropical climate. After all, Galveston Harbor had been known to freeze during the winter, but in 1936, early February temperatures remained in the seventies and even topped eighty degrees. To the contrary, just one thousand miles north, bitter cold gripped all of Chicago and the Upper Midwest. At one point, the temperature did not rise above zero for 273 hours, and when Moody arrived in town around February 17, daytime highs remained in the single digits, with a constant twenty-mile-an-hour wind creating a wind chill of five to ten degrees below zero in the warmest part of the day. Shearn Moody traveled from one extreme to the other, and his body was not prepared for the change.

Some Moody detractors have chosen to place the blame for Shearn's bout with pneumonia on Shearn himself. Accounts claim he traveled northward unprepared for the cold weather, which is certainly possible considering the unseasonable weather in Galveston. But those same accounts claim that upon arriving in Chicago, Moody was too thrifty or "frugal," as his grandfather would have said, to spend money on an overcoat. Whether or not the stories are true, the fact remains that upon arriving back in Galveston, Moody immediately came down with a severe respiratory infection that quickly turned into pneumonia. Doctors also diagnosed him with influenza, and his condition deteriorated to the point that he was placed in an oxygen tent.

In 1934, the advent of antibiotics remained in its infancy. Clinical testing had shown great promise, but it would be another ten years before the medicines became widely available. Shearn Moody's physicians had few tools to treat pneumonia other than an oxygen tent and hope. Hope faded when Moody slipped into a coma. In the early morning hours of February 28, Shearn Moody died with his wife, Frances, at his bedside. In Moody's death at just forty years old, Galveston lost one of its most influential and civic-minded citizens, one on whom many counted to lead the city and his family's business interests into the later half of the twentieth century.

The Moodys wasted little time in planning Shearn's funeral. As Galveston city offices and businesses lowered their flags to half-mast, the

SHEARN MOODY

1895-1936

BEYOND THE LAST HORIZON'S RIM
BEYOND ADVENTURE'S FARTHEST QUEST,
SOMEWHERE THEY RISE, SERENE AND DIM,
THE HAPPY, HAPPY HILLS OF REST.

—ALBERT BIGELOW PAINE

Shearn Moody, 1895–1936. *Courtesy E. Douglas McLeod/Moody Archives.*

Shearn Moody moved into this residence at 16 Cedar Lawn Circle in 1931. *Courtesy of E. Douglas McLeod/Moody Archives.*

Moodys hastily arranged to inter Shearn's body in the family mausoleum at Galveston Memorial Park. The cemetery, located several miles inland near Hitchcock, held the remains of several prominent islanders who died in the early twentieth century. Too many families remembered the aftermath of the 1900 hurricane, when flooding had exhumed coffins and scattered them across the island. On Saturday, March 1, 1936, following a funeral service at his home on Cedar Lawn Circle, a hearse carried Shearn Moody to his final resting place. Longtime friend and associate Roy Koehler served as a pallbearer.

Shearn Moody offered Bill Van Fleet his first job in the newspaper business, and the sportswriter devoted his Saturday column to memorializing Moody. He took special care to dispel any notion that Moody had pressured him to write only positive stories about the Buccaneers. While many questioned whether Van Fleet's predecessor had suffered Moody's wrath in his hasty exit from the *GDN*, Van Fleet unequivocally denied Shearn Moody had ever directed his work as a journalist. As Van Fleet wrote in his "Here's the Dope" column the day after Shearn's death:

> *It is easy to compliment the dead. The kindly virtues are remembered and many deeds that might be extolled pass before the mind's eye.*

In this connection it would be a simple thing to fill this column and several others talking about the things Shearn Moody did for Galveston sport fans, the Texas League and baseball in general.

Instead, there is something we have wanted to say for a long time. On occasions, we have decided that someday when the time came to leave Galveston and this paper and move somewhere else, that the final "Dope" column should be about this same subject. There could be no doubt about its sincerity then, and there can be none now.

***

Not one time, but many times, fans have said to the writer, "You should take this player or that player to task in your column, but I know you dare not. Shearn wouldn't allow you to talk about his ball club."

How far from the truth! Shearn Moody never told this writer not to criticise [sic] the Galveston Ball Club. He never objected when one player or another was singled out for criticism. He might never had read this column for all th[at] he said about it concerning the…performances of the ballplayers. In better than four years of writing for this paper, the writer never had one expression from Shearn as to what to say or think in this column.

And that is more than you can say for dozens of others who have been connected with sports one way or another in this city.

***

Then again, there was the fallacy that scorers in Galveston were lenient with the home team because Shearn liked to see the averages run high. Disgruntled fans were apt to express this opinion when the home team lost and some player who helped lose it was credited with a scratch hit. The writer has heard such opinions expressed.

The only time he ever said anything one way or another about a hit or an error, so far as the writer knows, was in Houston after the opening game of 1935. Charlie English had hit a scratchy infield bounder [d]own the first base line and was safe after the ball had been juggled. It was a hit, for he had the play beat, and the official scorer ruled it so.

After the game Shearn said: "You fellows give those players a hit on any kind of a ball. I never would have given English a hit on that play tonight."

***

Then there was the time when the writer saw him in a café. He pulled a letter from his pocket, and handed it over along with an attached clipping.

The clipping was from this column, containing the suggestion that ballplayers in the Texas League should be in on a percentage of the gate receipts during the Shaughessy playoffs.

The letter was from another Texas League club owner and it was a bitter protest against the Galveston president letting the local newspaper talk of splitting any of the Shaughnessy playoff receipts.

"I thought you would want to see this," Shearn said. "But don't pay any attention to it.

***

Another time an official of a major league club felt that he was not complimented by something said in this column. He wrote a letter of protest—not to the writer but to Shearn Moody, who was financially interested in both the newspaper and the ball club. It was a bitter letter, not very complimentary to either this writer or any other sportswriter.

Some two months after he received the letter, the president of the Bucs placed it in an envelope and mailed it to the sports desk, with the notation, "Thought you might be interested."

Personally, we always felt he agreed with what was written and we would like to have seen the answer he sent the major league official.

***

And again there was the time, after he became interested in building the Moody Club girls basket ball team into contenders for the state championship, when the suggestion was made to him that he could have a certain star off a rival team if he would give her a job. The star player would have led the Ramblers into certain city championship winners and probable state winners.

"I'm not interested," he said. "She's playing for a rival team and if we can't beat her without taking her away from them, we don't want to win.

***

The above incidents are from personal experience, seen from some four years working on his newspaper.

***

What he did for baseball and the Texas League is known to most people connected with the sport. He came to the league when the Depression had it on the run. Tyler, Longview, Wichita Falls, Shreveport, Waco—those towns that baseball could not be made to pay. Other franchise owners were disgusted. He lent some solid financial backing then with Roy Koehler started injecting sound business methods into the sport that allowed it to live. Other club owners, not only in the Texas League, but elsewhere, abided by some of these innovations. Few know just how desperately his "push" was needed by the Texas League back in 1931, 1932 and 1933.

***

Baseball, and in the last year all sports, was his hobby. He was a fan, with those affiliated with him in the Texas League often using that term as a reproach when arguments over umpires, players and the game became warm. He wanted to win, and he so keenly wanted to win he would argue all night to gain his point.

At the end of the 1934 season when he was selling eight ball players to the big league from the local club, he [missing word] in each sale because he was doing something every other Texas League club owner wanted to do—and doing it on a hitherto unequalled scale. He was winning.

Later he told the writer: "I'm through with selling ballplayers. After this I'm going to try to get a good club and keep it."

The draft, of course, would never have let him do so.

***

There will never be another Shearn Moody backing a ball club. He lent that sport the same zeal, the same engaging energy and the same attention to details that characterized his every other venture. He made it go.

After the 1937 season, Bill Van Fleet left Galveston for Fort Worth and began a long career with the *Star-Telegram*. His daughter, Mary Van Fleet Williams, confirms her father as a professional journalist who wrote either the truth or his own opinions, never leaving the reader to question fact versus conjecture: "Daddy was well known, respected and beloved by many. He wrote with integrity and fairness, always interested in promoting his love of sports rather than digging up dirt."

When legendary Texas Longhorn football coach Darrell Royal decided to retire in 1976, the only member of the media he notified in advance was Bill Van Fleet, by then sports editor of the *Star-Telegram*: "Daddy had that good a reputation. Darrell Royal was about to make a huge announcement and wanted to keep it a secret, but he trusted and respected Daddy enough to let him know in advance."

Following Shearn's death, Will Moody became despondent. Not only had he lost a son and his best friend, but he also lost a business advisor and the future patriarch of the Moody enterprises. Now seventy years old, Will realized no other family member had been prepared to take over upon his death. He brought Shearn's older sister, Mary Moody Northen, into his inner circle and successfully educated her in the ways of finance.

Some claims of Shearn Moody as a heartless, hard-driving businessman may have merit; in fact, many thought the same of a young Will Moody. As he aged, Will grew less stern and more interested in both his immediate and extended family—employees of Moody business holdings. Written accounts of Shearn's behavior in his final few years—playfully socializing with employees at Moody business picnics, supporting his father in not laying off a single employee despite the severe economic hardships of the Great Depression and becoming the doting father of a three-year-old and a newborn son—he, too, may have begun to soften. While no one knows what Shearn Moody might have accomplished had he lived a full life, he undoubtedly held many aspirations.

Within days of Moody's death, the family faced decisions about the future of Shearn's pet project, the Galveston Buccaneers. With players due to report in only two weeks, the family stated publicly that they would continue to field the baseball team and placed Roy Koehler in charge of the franchise. Privately, no Moody shared Shearn's interest in baseball, and few bought into his expectations that the Buccaneers would help fill Moody hotels.

After 1935's playoff appearance, Jack Mealey returned as Galveston's manager with a severely depleted roster. Buck Fausett and Charlie English had both moved on, and the only remaining players from the 1934 championship team included Tony Governor, Jim McLeod, Sig Jakucki and Joe Gibbs. While Billy Webb had held his roster together and used few players over the course of the season, in 1936, the Bucs' roster expanded. Twenty-four players, including twelve pitchers, appeared on the roster. Only Joe Gibbs's 15-15 record offered any semblance of success, however, and the overall team batting average plummeted. Outfielder Jimmy Moore led the team at .288, with fellow outfielders Chuck Hostetler and Tony Governor trailing in the .270s. The rest of the lineup contributed little to a mediocre offense, hitting only sixteen home runs and few extra-base hits on the season. Not surprisingly, a poor offense coupled with a rising ERA among the pitching staff led to a disappointing season. Jake Atz replaced Mealey as manager, but Atz had no more success, and the Buccaneers finished last in the standings with just fifty-seven wins.

Much speculation surrounded the Buccaneers' future. The Moodys quietly sought to dispose of their ownership, but they did not want to cease operations in deference to still-devoted fans. Shreveport lobbied for the team, but a deal never materialized. The Bucs headed into 1937 with new

The 1936 Galveston Buccaneers fought on even after the death of team owner Shearn Moody. *Courtesy of Robert J. Fausett.*

manager Hank Severeid, whom they had faced as a San Antonio Mission in the playoffs of 1933 and 1934.

At forty-six years old, Severeid played sporadically, appearing in nearly forty games. With Tony Governor returning to form, the team's hitting improved, but the Bucs' pitching staff had aged, with three regularly used hurlers approaching forty years old. Ed Cole led the staff with an 18-18 record, while Jim Bivin returned and claimed seven wins. But the team ERA ballooned above 4.00. The 1937 Buccaneers ultimately fared slightly better than in 1936, finishing in sixth place.

After two unsuccessful seasons, local fans lost interest in the Buccaneers. Without Shearn Moody's interest, few believed the family would make an effort to field a competitive team, and attendance fell. Shearn Moody's estate could no longer justify owning the Buccaneers and set out in search of a buyer.

Though the Moodys wanted the Buccaneers to remain in Galveston, they found no interested buyers. Shreveport, though, remained in search of a Texas League franchise, and after weeks of negotiations, Shearn Moody's estate quietly sold the Buccaneers to Shreveport investors. Upon moving to Louisiana, the new owners renamed their team the Shreveport Sports and had a two-year-old ballpark awaiting the franchise's arrival. Forty-nine years after the Texas League originally began play, and with

Galveston a league member for forty-three of those seasons, the Texas League left Galveston for good. Professional baseball did not return to the island until 1950, when the Galveston White Caps played five seasons in the Gulf Coast and Big State Leagues.

As for Moody Stadium, the former crown jewel of Texas League ballparks, a tropical storm severely damaged the structure a year after the Buccaneers left town. Galveston razed the structure to make way for a public housing project.

Today, the ten-acre site once occupied by Moody Stadium and thousands of rowdy baseball fans sits empty, completely surrounded by a locked chain-link fence. Few recall that the finest team Galveston ever fielded called the site home in 1934, when, for one splendid season, Shearn Moody's Galveston Buccaneers represented the class of the Texas League.

AFTERWORD

Cincinnati, Ohio, April 10, 1944

When Buck Fausett declared his loyalty to Shearn Moody in turning down Connie Mack's contract offer in 1935, he probably didn't realize he might have passed on his only chance at the Major Leagues. But by 1944, with World War II in its third year, quality players to fill out big-league rosters became hard to find. Fausett toiled for twelve years in the minors, yet he seemed to improve with age. A reliable third baseman, Buck batted as high as .339 in his five years in the American Association, and he had his best two professional seasons while playing with the Little Rock Travelers as he entered his mid-thirties.

In Little Rock, just a short drive from his birthplace in Grant County, Fausett finished second in the 1942 Southern Association batting race with a .334 average. He also led the league at third base with 307 assists and a .946 fielding average. His play, along with that of former Galveston teammate Bill McGhee, carried Little Rock to the pennant.

When Travelers manager Willis Hudlin enlisted in the U.S. Air Corps after the 1942 season, Fausett's experience and talent made him a natural choice to serve as player-manager. At thirty-five years old, he posted a career-best .362 average, gathering 205 hits in just 140 games. His fielding held steady, and for the second consecutive season, Fausett turned over three hundred assists at third base. The Travelers didn't repeat as league champions, but Buck still led them to a third-place finish.

Despite his age, Cincinnati Reds manager Bill McKechnie finally took note of Fausett's skills. Short an infielder and a left-handed batter, he signed

Buck Fausett. *Courtesy of Robert J. Fausett.*

Buck to his first major-league contract. Buck Fausett made his debut as a thirty-six-year-old rookie on opening day in 1944.

"Physically, I'm probably past my peak," Fausett said. "But at the age of thirty-six I've picked up a lot of baseball savvy that can be put to good use."

Buck sat on the bench for the majority of the opener with the Chicago Cubs, but with two outs in the ninth inning, he had his first major-league at-bat. Unfortunately, no fairy tale lay in store. Fausett flied out to end the game, a 3–0 loss for the Reds. Eight games later, he broke into the starting lineup against Pittsburgh.

Buck didn't get a hit against the Pirates, but he did drive in a run on a fielder's choice in a 2–0 Reds victory. A day later, he recorded his first major-league hit, a triple, in a 7–3 loss. Fausett started the next six games, reaching base only three times in twenty-four at-bats.

On June 1, 1944, Reds manager Bill McKechnie placed Fausett on the mound in a relief role against the Phillies in what may have been his first pitching appearance since college. Buck pitched well, allowing just two runs over four innings. Ten days later, he pitched again with the Reds already trailing the Cardinals 7–0 in the second inning. He lasted six innings, allowing six runs on ten hits and also picking up a hit of his own. In the ninth inning, McKechnie replaced Fausett with Joe Nuxhall, a fifteen-year-old high school standout who joined the team for the summer. Nuxhall walked five and allowed five runs in his only game of the season. The schoolboy became the youngest player to appear in the Major Leagues, a record he still holds today. Ironically, when Nuxhall relieved Fausett, it marked the first appearance of a sixteen-year career, as well as the end of Fausett's brief stay in the big leagues. Less than a week later, the Reds sold Fausett to the Hollywood Stars of the Pacific Coast League.

In Hollywood, Fausett became a fan favorite, batting .315 in each of his two seasons, the second of which he managed and played third base. When the Stars finished with a 73-100 record on the long West Coast season, fans began to grumble. A year later, Fausett left the team after eighty-four games. No one was more disappointed than Anne Fausett when the family left Hollywood for Albuquerque in the West Texas–New Mexico League. Anne grew used to the Hollywood lifestyle and thoroughly enjoyed socializing with stars like the Marx Brothers and John Wayne. Buck, on the other hand, barely knew any celebrity's name and anxiously joined the Albuquerque Dukes, a team he and his cousin purchased in the off season. Fausett finished 1947 with the Dukes, batting .439 in nineteen appearances. A year later, he posted an astounding .409 average in 545 at-bats and drove in 140 runs, with career highs in doubles, triples and home runs. The high plains and dry air of West Texas and New Mexico truly made the league a hitter's paradise.

At season's end, Fausett sold his interest in the Dukes, signing on as manager and part owner of the Amarillo Gold Sox after turning down the San Antonio Missions manager's position. Now forty years old, Buck drove in over one hundred runs for the Gold Sox, earned All-Star honors and tied in voting for Manager of the Year.

After the 1948 season, Buck retired as a player. In eighteen professional seasons, he appeared in 2,262 games, collected 2,677 base hits and posted a .310 batting average. Though he no longer played, Buck and baseball could not be separated. In 1949, he managed the Gold Sox to the championship series, after which he sold his share of the club. Over the next seven years, he served in the front offices of Amarillo and Albuquerque, also managing the Dukes in 1952.

In his final season as a manager, Buck purchased the contract of Herbert Simpson, an African American first baseman who began his career in the Negro Leagues. Simpson played three seasons for the Dukes, batting .344 in 1952. Despite challenges he faced as just the second African American player in the West Texas–New Mexico League, Simpson recalled the kindness of his manager. When a heckler in Amarillo got out of hand, Fausett sent a couple of players to have a private chat with the gentleman beneath the grandstand. A few minutes later, the three returned, the bloodied heckler quietly taking his seat and remaining silent for the rest of the game. When playing in Borger, Texas, that same season, the Dukes checked into the team's usual motel. Fausett soon received a call from the manager requesting that Herb Simpson stay elsewhere, as his presence upset other guests. Herb did move to an integrated motel directly across the street, as did Buck and

Buck Fausett and family, circa 1940. *Courtesy of Robert J. Fausett.*

Fausett's grave in Hopkins County. *Karen Rutherford.*

Simpson's teammates. As word of the motel's service and restaurant spread, it soon provided accommodations for all baseball teams visiting Borger.

In 1957, Buck Fausett finally left baseball for good, some thirty years after he first appeared in organized ball at East Texas Teachers College. He and Anne returned to Galveston, and Buck worked in sales until the early 1970s, when the couple moved to College Station, where Robert Jr. attended veterinary school. In 1983, they mourned the untimely death of their only child, remaining in College Station to help raise their grandsons.

Robert recalls his grandfather as a man who seldom spoke of baseball, despite his long, successful professional career. On May 2, 1994, Buck died at the age of eighty-six; his wife, Anne, passed away two years later. The couple rests alongside their son and Buck's parents near Sulphur Springs, just a few miles from the Hopkins County farm that Buck Fausett had worked so hard to escape.

SOURCES

PERSONAL INTERVIEWS AND CORRESPONDENCE

Stanford Elbert
Robert Fausett
Scott Hanzelka
Tom Kayser
E. Douglas McLeod
Bobby Moody Jr.
Mary Mowlam
Dianne Sides
Mary Van Fleet Williams

ARCHIVES

Rosenberg Library, Galveston and Texas History Center

WEBSITES

Ancestry.com
Baseball-Reference.com, www.baseball-reference.com.
Encyclopedia of Arkansas History and Culture, www.encyclopediaofarkansas.com.

SOURCES

Library of Congress, www.memory.loc.gov.
National Weather Service, www.noaa.gov.
NewspaperArchive.com
Portal to Texas History, www.texashistory.unt.edu.
Sanford Fire Maps, www.lib.utexas.edu.
Society for American Baseball Research, www.sabr.org.

NEWSPAPERS AND PERIODICALS

American Monthly Review of Reviews (July 1903)
Chicago Tribune
Daily Oklahoman
Dallas Morning News
Fort Worth Star-Telegram
Galveston Daily News
Galveston Tribune
House of Moody
Houston Chronicle
Paris News
San Antonio Light

SPORTING LIFE

Reach's Baseball Guide
Spalding's Baseball Guide

BOOKS AND MANUSCRIPTS

Barnhart, Jeff. *The Longview Cannibals: A Complete History of East Texas' Most Celebrated Baseball Club.* Lufkin: Best of East Texas Publishers, 2009.

Bodley, Hal. *How Baseball Explains America.* Chicago: Triumph Books, 2014.

Cartwright, Gary. *Galveston: A History of the Island.* Forth Worth, TX: TCU Press, 1991.

SOURCES

Greene, Casey Edward, and Shelly Henley Kelly. *Through a Night of Horrors: Voices from the 1900 Galveston Storm.* College Station: Texas A&M University Press, 2000.

Johnson, Lloyd, and Miles Wolff. *Encyclopedia of Minor League Baseball.* 3rd ed. Durham, NC: Baseball America, 2007.

Kayser, Tom, and David King. *The Texas League Baseball Almanac.* Charleston, SC: The History Press, 2014.

———. *The Texas League's Greatest Hits: Baseball in the Lone Star State.* San Antonio, TX: Trinity University Press, 2005.

Kirsch, George B. *Baseball in Blue and Gray: The National Pastime During the Civil War.* Princeton, NJ: Princeton University Press, 2003.

McComb, David G. *Galveston: A History.* Austin: University of Texas Press, 1986.

———. *Spare Time in Texas: Recreation and History in the Lone Star State.* Austin: University of Texas Press, 2008.

O'Neal, Bill. *The Texas League, 1888–1987: A Century of Baseball.* Austin, TX: Eakin Press, 1987.

Ruggles, William B. "The History of the Texas League of Professional Baseball Clubs: 1888–1951." Texas League, 1951.

Rutherford, Kris. *Baseball on the Prairie: How Seven Small-Town Teams Shaped Texas League History.* Charleston, SC: The History Press, 2014.

Texas League of Baseball Clubs. *2013 Media Guide and Record Book.* San Antonio: Texas League, 2013.

Vaught, David. *The Farmers' Game: Baseball in Rural America.* Baltimore, MD: Johns Hopkins University Press, 2013.

Walker, Mike. *SPV's Comprehensive Railroad Atlas of North America: Texas.* Kent, UK: Ian Andrews, 2001.

SOURCES

Weems, John Edward. *A Weekend in September*. College Station: Texas A&M University Press, 1980.

Wright, Marshall D. *The Texas League in Baseball: 1858–1958*. Jefferson, NC: McFarland and Company, 2004.

INDEX

INDEX

INDEX

ABOUT THE AUTHOR

Kris Rutherford has been writing professionally in some capacity since 1989. This is his third book on Texas League Baseball history, and he has published two middle-grade sports novels. He provides historical content for the *Texas League Newsletter*, published on MiLB.com. He currently works full time as a grant writer in Arkansas. He and his wife, Karen, are publishers of the Lamar County, Texas newspaper the *Roxton Progress*.

www.krisrutherford.com

Kris Rutherford (right) with E. Douglas McLeod. *Photo by Karen Rutherford.*

Visit us at
www.historypress.net

This title is also available as an e-book

Printed in the USA
CPSIA information can be obtained
at www.ICGtesting.com
LVHW020000080923
757498LV00037B/8

9 781540 212801